# To Market, To Market

# To Market,

**The Public Market Tradition in Canada**

**by Linda Biesenthal**

**photographs by J. Douglas Wilson**

# To Market

**PMA Books**

**Canadian Cataloguing in Publication Data**

Biesenthal, Linda, 1950-
    To market, to market

Bibliography: p.
ISBN 0-88778-207-8 bd.

1. Markets- Canada - History. 2. Farm produce -
Canada - Marketing. 3. Markets.   I. Title.

HF5472.C3B53    381'.18'0971    C80-094469-0

Design: Michael Solomon

PETER MARTIN ASSOCIATES LIMITED
280 Bloor Street West, Toronto, Canada M5S 1W1

# Contents

# Preface

I knew nothing about the public market tradition when I started this project. Most of what I now know was gathered, amid the tomatoes and turnips, in long, animated conversations with the market people of Canada. They were delighted that someone was interested and willingly passed on generations of gossip, and insightful, forthright opinions. I am indebted to them all, and especially to Mary Ann LaPierre, Joyce LaPierre, Mr. T. Choma, Olga and Victor Pleshko, Johanna Earthrowl, Stirling Wood, Mrs. B. K. Ferguson, Mr. and Mrs. David Mutch, Ken Harris and Pat Nealis. The provincial departments of agriculture and the provincial and city archives provided additional information.

I bravely and naively began this project completely on my own. Without the special help and gentle coercion of the following people I would never have finished it: Doug Wilson, Carol Martin, Kathy Vanderlinden, Larry Biesenthal, Michael Solomon, Yvonne Grue, Eleanor and Doug Spence, and Leona and Robert Alexander. And without the generous financial support of the Ontario Arts Council I could not have started it.

*To Market, To Market* is dedicated to Carol Martin, a friend every writer should have, and to Canada's market people, whose story it has been a pleasure to pass on.

# The Market Tradition

OUR ancestors became farmers about ten thousand years ago. When families first settled down together in communities to begin systematically cultivating the soil and grazing livestock, each family grew, raised and made everything it needed to survive. Eventually neighbours began to barter. One family made better stools and made them faster, another always managed to raise more ducks than it could consume, and another family was able to weave four times as much cloth as anyone else. When his family needed cloth, the man skillful at making stools would travel perhaps a whole day to trade a stool for a piece of cloth. But he might find at the end of his long journey that the expert weaver was off trading cloth for ducks, or even worse, that the weaver did not want to trade because he had been swindled four days earlier and had no ducks or cloth to barter.

Obviously a better way had to be found for neighbours to exchange goods. When there were enough people in a community with assorted talents and things to trade, someone would propose that everyone gather at a spot and time convenient to all. This gathering together of many buyers and sellers in one place at the same time was the community's first market.

Few things were traded in these very early markets. Everyone shared the same attitude toward trading: it was a last resort. People worried first about what they could produce for themselves and secondly, and reluctantly, what they could get exchanging with neighbours. Farmers in the community did not trade for profit; they exchanged necessities only in order to subsist.

Though profit was not a motive in these markets, petty deceit was common. Short measures were given and unwholesome food sometimes sold. If a farmer needed two ducks to trade for a bushel of grain and he had one healthy duck and another that had died mysteriously the day before,

he plucked them both, took them to market and hoped his neighbour would be fooled. Mutual distrust was the only protection. It soon became clear that honesty would not prevail until it was institutionalized, until rules and penalties were established to discourage people from unfair dealing. Then an official had to be appointed to check weights and measures and the quality of goods offered for sale, to enforce the rules and to punish offenders.

The first markets were held in the open air because there was nothing else available. They continued to be held in the open to protect buyers. If everything were bought and sold in plain view, sellers would be discouraged from deceiving their customers.

Deception did not suddenly disappear. The standard of morality in the markets of ancient Greece was notoriously low. In the seventh century B.C. a Greek writer described the market as "a place set apart where men deceive one another". Markets had been operating for thousands of years when Hesiod offered his golden market rule: "In any and every transaction, though it be with your own brother, call witness—but do it with a pleasant smile." Mutual distrust was still the best protection.

The Greeks and Romans had more than petty deceivers to worry about. Profiteers who bought cheap and sold dear, and speculators who hoarded supplies to enhance the price had operated in the earlier markets. But they had never been denounced as much as they were in Greece and Rome. Aristotle condemned profiteering as an unnatural act. It was considered wrong to profit from others' needs, from the buying and selling of essential goods.

Profit was introduced in the Greek and Roman markets by merchants and traders. They made their living travelling from one country, colony, city or market to the next, buying goods that were plentiful and cheap in one place and selling them in another where they were scarce and expensive.

Those who took risks and transported their wares over a long distance were tolerated, especially if they carried essential commodities such as grain. But small-time retailers who travelled no more than a hundred yards—buying at one end of the market to resell at the other—were condemned as especially loathsome creatures because they practiced petty tricks for petty gains.

Farmers, craftsmen and tradesmen who bought and sold in the markets expected no more than a just price for their goods—no more than it had cost to produce them. Everyone in the market knew the just price of a goat or other commonly traded commodities. It was much more difficult to assess the just price of goods imported by merchants and traders. Their dealings in the market were therefore scrupulously watched and strictly regulated.

Markets in Greece and Rome were established to benefit everyone in the community equally. Market rules and regulations were devised to ensure that an ample supply of goods, especially food, was available at a just price. This required tight control. To ensure the supervision of all market commerce the Roman state assumed the sole right to establish and regulate markets. One important restriction was that markets in neighbouring towns could not be held on the same day so as not to interfere with local supply and demand.

The rules and attitudes governing market trade in Rome and Greece (and elsewhere) travelled to Europe probably with the merchants and traders and with pioneering colonists. The idea of a just price, the prerogative of the king to create and regulate markets, and the distrust of the profiteering middleman reappeared in the medieval markets.

During the Middle Ages officials went one step further in regulating their markets. To curtail private dealing (an easy way to take advantage of consumers) it was forbidden to buy or sell outside the market or before the market opened. This rule applied to everyone, even the craftsmen and tradesmen who sold their wares from small shops at the front of their houses. In 1299 the Market Master of Worms proclaimed that "all shoemakers in the buying and selling of their shoes must go to the public market or where they are being ordered and no one is allowed to sell shoes on market days anywhere else, not in his house or under his house gates in any way". In a small English town in the late Middle Ages no one was to "open either sak, pooke . . . or any other vessell wherein victualls or other things be" before the morning market bell was rung.

Restricting trade to the markets was the only way of enforcing the complex series of rules and regulations that had been devised to protect consumers. It was also the only way of ensuring that all buyers and sellers had full knowledge of market supply and demand. And it appeared to be the only way of introducing standardized weights and measures.

In England in 1215 the Magna Carta proclaimed that hereafter "there shall be one measure of wine throughout our realm, and one measure of ale, and one measure of corn, namely the London Quarter . . . and as with measures, so with weights". Despite this declaration people continued to sell by "aime of hand" and to rely on their own good sense for the size of a bushel. Eventually, centuries after the signing of the Magna Carta, the king appointed a Master Weigher of the Realm whose job it was to travel from market to market checking for correct weights and measures. Standardization came, but it came slowly and against great resistance. When it was first enforced in the Bury St. Edmonds market, buyers and sellers fled to another town which still had weights and measures they were accustomed to. Apparently the Master Weigher had not been there yet.

The market had its heyday in the market towns of the late Middle Ages. Merchants made these towns their headquarters and usually became prominent, powerful citizens. Artisans settled permanently in these towns to manufacture goods specifically to sell for profit in the market and annual fair.° Farmers from the surrounding countryside also benefited from all this commercial and industrial activity, and they too began producing things to sell for a profit in the market. On market days merchants and artisans came to the marketplace with their shoes, cloaks, cooking utensils, swords, salt, pepper, beer, wine, bread, candles, tools and farm implements; country people arrived with wool, hides, pigs, ducks, geese, chickens, grain, butter, eggs, wax and honey. The town economy had emerged, with people making, producing and exchanging their goods for profit.

As populations increased and grew denser, as transportation became easier, as farmers became better farmers and tradesmen more specialized, and as a demand arose for more goods and more luxury goods, continuous daily trade in shops and stores began to replace weekly trade in markets. In the early eighteenth century an Englishman was complaining that "the fairs and markets are becoming strangely thin; and where one can see little else besides toy-shops and stalls for bawbles and knicknacks. In some of them (cities, towns and other places of trade), the markets are entirely left off and disused, as if the town had lost its character. The tolls sunk to nothing . . . and in some boroughs . . . now grass grows in the market-place."

Farmers were concentrating on producing greater quantities of grain and raising more and better livestock, especially after the agricultural revolution that began in the seventeenth century. It left them little time, or inclination, to prepare and transport goods to the market and spend all day there selling them. Tradesmen were too busy manufacturing to hunt through the market for raw materials. Wholesalers appeared to act as agents for both producers and consumers.

The traditional form of exchange was being transformed. Producers and consumers were no longer meeting face-to-face. The middleman now controlled a large corner of the food trade.

The markets did not disappear, but they were certainly replaced by a more efficient food distribution system. Many towns continued to provide an open square where farmers and consumers could meet. Town officials, still holding onto some of their traditional attitudes about trade, considered these markets to be a check on collusion between private dealers. In larger cities and towns many markets were turned over to wholesalers. Others continued to operate as they had for centuries, but at a slower pace.

The market tradition is the set of customs, rules, attitudes and beliefs that governed the way our ancestors exchanged life's necessities. This tradition has been passed down for thousands of years from one generation to the next and carried over thousands of miles by merchants and colonists. Markets throughout history have shared three essential features: they are open to all buyers and sellers in the community; they handle local trade and mostly food; and they are regulated and supervised to ensure that consumers are protected from unscrupulous sellers.

° Annual fairs were held throughout medieval Europe to attract long-distance traders and merchants with imported necessities and luxuries to sell. The fair has been called "the occasion of greatest freedom in medieval economy". In most towns and cities in Europe during the Middle Ages merchants and craftsmen had formed guilds, and only members of the guilds were allowed to sell in local markets. But anyone could sell at the fair, and almost everyone did. Fairs assembled together traders, merchants and shopkeepers who bought goods specifically to resell. Set out in open air stalls were bales of English wool, Flemish linens, French wines, exotic silks and velvets, barrels of salted fish, tools and implements. Farmers and craftsmen from neighbouring towns brought cattle, grain, homespun cloth, shoes, and pots and pans. These fairs were occasions for selling large quantities and making bulk purchases of items such as salt, spices, tallow, rushes and sweet-smelling herbs for strewing on the cottage floor. They were also occasions for revelling and carousing.

Though most importantly an economic institution, the market has always been much more than that. The marketplace has from the beginning been the community's social and cultural centre. As much gossip as grain has been exchanged in marketplaces. Political uprisings have germinated there. In marketplaces everywhere duels have been fought, scandals uncovered, ideas and skills exchanged, and men and women punished in the pillory.

There is now a public market renaissance. Our ancestors' attitudes about the middleman have come back to haunt: he is as unpopular now as he was six hundred years ago. At least four middlemen, and more likely six or seven, stand between the grain in farmers' fields and the bread on supermarket shelves. Consumers are turning to public markets in order to deal once again directly with producers, hoping to buy fresher food at cheaper prices.

The prices are usually not as cheap as consumers expect. The notion of a just price no longer operates. Farmers sell their fruit and vegetables and eggs for a profit, and usually they are satisfied with a reasonable one. Their prices match current wholesale prices, or undercut them by a penny or two.

Farmers and craftsmen as well as consumers are being attracted back to the marketplace where the community gathers as much as to the market where the community trades. In the market they enjoy a very personal and high-spirited form of commerce. In the marketplace they enjoy the pleasures of community. And everyone enjoys the market's special atmosphere. That sense of stepping back into an older and apparently simpler world strikes most of us as soon as we enter a market. Its noisy chaos—vendors shouting out their prices and customers haggling for better ones; its curious smells—a blend of fresh onions, fresh fish, fresh bread and fresh air; and its energetic activity—robust, suntanned farmers hefting crates of cabbages from their trucks to their stalls, and buxom, kerchiefed women building pyramids of ripe tomatoes—all seem to belong to another time and place.

# 1 Early Markets

THE market probably made its first appearance sometime around 4000 B.C. in the farming communities clustered together in the fertile Nile Valley. By then the ancient Egyptians had become accomplished farmers, capable of producing almost three times the amount of food their families needed. Some of their villages had grown into towns and cities with their own gods, their own rulers, their own artisans, labourers, priests and appointed officials, and their own markets.

It was hard to distinguish between buyers and sellers in these early markets. Except for the occasional trader or merchant, everyone in the market was a producer. They all congregated in an open spot in the centre of town, laden down with the things they had brought from their homes, gardens and workshops to trade in the market. Some of them displayed their wares on the ground, others carried them about in sacks flung around their necks.

Bartering in these markets required skill and perseverence. A buyer first had to find a vendor willing to barter for what he had to offer. This was not always easy. When buyer and seller met they took stock of each other, looking for weak spots. There was no currency in the market and no standardized weights to simplify the transaction. They had nothing to rely on but their ability to haggle and their willingness to compromise. After a vigorous debate and some boisterous name-calling, concessions were usually made.

These early markets appeared unruly, but some regulations must have been devised to keep them operating regularly and at least one supervisor appointed to maintain a measure of harmony in the marketplace. But no records exist to give an accurate description of these markets and of how they were administered. Nothing until about 3000 B.C. when scribes and artists began recording the activities of the market.

The scenes carved on a tomb found at Sakkarah depict a marketplace of the Old Kingdom (2780-2250 B.C.). Here peasants, craftsmen and labourers of a prosperous estate and the landlord's servants met several times a week to barter. After a slow journey from the distant countryside a peasant reaches the open square early and finds trade in the market already brisk. His shopping list is short. Bread, beer and onions are the staples of his family's diet. He passes a woman earnestly thrusting her pots of ointment under the nose of an old vendor selling jars of thick barley beer. Behind them another buyer, her trading goods still hidden away in a box, tries to make a deal with a fishmonger, who glances up occasionally from the great sheath-fish he is cleaning to extoll the merits of his catch. The peasant stops first to inspect a rush basket full of vegetables. While the seller examines the small necklace of stringed beads offered in exchange for a sack of onions, another prospective buyer interrupts to propose a better trade—a wooden fan for the same sack of onions. His onions purchased and stowed away, the peasant moves on to confer with a baker selling small loaves of raised bread. The baker protests that the worn leather collar the peasant extends for his inspection is worth no more than a single loaf of his fine bread. The peasant is finally satisfied when he has exchanged his collar for three loaves of a less appetizing flatbread. By the time he sets off homeward, he has also traded three fishhooks for a jug of oil, half a basket of wheat for a linen skirt and the other half for a small box of figs.

As market activity, and business generally, increased, Egyptian officials began to worry about devising a system for assessing the value of goods. The *shat* was introduced sometime during the second millenium. Although most Egyptians knew what weight of gold, silver or copper was equal to it, the *shat* was a purely imaginary measure. When neighbouring estates exchanged a large surplus of grain for a herd of cattle, the value of the grain was presented in *shat*, which determined the number of cattle expected in trade. The *shat* did not solve enough problems to be wholeheartedly adopted in the marketplace. Nor did it make much headway in the business world, and it was gradually replaced by a system based on precise weights. The *deben* (worth about two and a half ounces of gold, silver or copper) simplified the market's more complex transactions. In the thirteenth century B.C. a scribe sold one of his oxen, valued at 130 *deben*, for a linen tunic worth 60 *deben*, ten sacks and three and a half bushels of grain worth 20 *deben*, some beads valued at 30 *deben* and two more tunics each worth 10 *deben*. The peasant,

who seldom made such complex trades, remained generally unaffected by all this. He continued to buy and sell in the market as he had done for years, determining the value of goods on the basis of how badly he needed them and haggling with the vendor until they agreed on a price.

For centuries very little changed in the markets that operated on the grand estates and in the small agricultural communities of Egypt, while those in the cities and larger towns, where life and commerce had become considerably more complex, were acquiring a new and different character. In the marketplace in Thebes in the fourteenth century B.C., long-distance traders and local merchants joined the farmers and craftsmen in the open square where the daily market was held. The local merchant made his living selling the basic necessities. In his stall bolts of cloth, sandals, baskets of produce, tanned hides, combs, sickles and pickaxes were all jumbled together. He was eager to trade and willing to accept almost anything in exchange. Set up alongside the merchant was the long-distance trader, who offered life's luxuries: Phoenician jewelry, lapis lazuli from Babylon and scented woods from southern Arabia. At the far end of the marketplace was the bazaar, three short, narrow streets lined with the permanent shops and stalls of bakers, carpenters, weavers and goldsmiths. After bartering for provisions in the market most shoppers passed through the bazaar to feast their eyes on gold bracelets and rows of pastries filled with honey and spices. They usually made two stops in the bazaar before turning homeward: at the cookshop to buy half a roasted duck to give them strength and at the tavern for a jar of beer to lighten their load.

Besides the farmer and craftsman the one other character who dominates the scenes of Egyptian marketplaces is the Master Weigher. By the twelfth century B.C. in a city like Thebes, most Egyptians were using rings of gold and silver or twisted wires of copper, called *outnou*, as payment in even

*A Master Weigher weighing gold rings. The weights are in the form of a cow's head, a lion and a cone.*

their simplest market transactions. Prosperous businessmen paid three *outnou* of gold for a leather flask of fine wine; a farmer paid a quarter of an *outnou* of copper for a pair of ducks. Each day, in full view of everyone in the market, the Master Weigher weighed the rings on the public scales set up at the entrance to the market. He assured vendors that the rings offered in payment contained the right amount of metal, and he unmasked swindlers who misrepresented the weight and quality of their *outnou*. The Master Weigher at his scales was a sign for all buyers and sellers that honesty prevailed in the market.

There does not appear to have been a complex code of laws regulating the activities of the ancient Egyptian markets. At least we have no record of one. The Egyptians were, however, concerned about morality in the marketplace. At least three of the moral declarations in the Book of the Dead, which deceased Egyptians recited when facing judgment by the great god Osiris, absolved them from the guilt of cheating in the market: "I have not diminished the bushel"; "I have not added to the weights of the scales"; "I have not misread the pointer of the scales."

These after-the-fact declarations obviously had little effect on market morality. It was the Greeks and the Romans who turned their formidable talents to bringing good government to the public market.

# 2 Markets in Ancient Athens and Rome

WE never think of the agora in Athens or the forum in Rome as the place where farmers brought their pigs to sell. Instead we have images of Socrates in long flowing robes discoursing with a student who has followed him to the agora, or of magnificent marble arches and columns in the Roman forum. But both began as simple, unadorned marketplaces when Athens and Rome were trading posts for the farms and villages nearby. By the sixth century B.C. each had become much more than a gathering place for buyers and sellers: the whole of public life was carried on there. Laws were passed, criminals tried and punished, gods worshipped, games and pageants played out and commerce transacted. Within their boundary stones, friends and rivals met to profess and argue their ideas on art, morality and politics. On a typical market day thieves rubbed shoulders with magistrates, and pedlars hawked their wares outside the treasury.

According to one Athenian writer this concentration of public business did not make a whit of difference to the character of the agora. It simply meant that there were more things to buy and sell:

You will find everything sold together in the same place in Athens: figs, witnesses to summonses, bunches of grapes, turnips, pears, apples, givers of evidence, roses, medlars, porridge, honey-combs, chick-peas, law-suits, beestings-puddings, myrtle, allotment-machines, irises, water-clocks, laws, indictments.[1]

More than one prominent Athenian complained about the mixing of civic and commercial business. Aristotle, always wary about how easily the profit motive could taint public affairs, suggested that a separate agora should be set up for the exclusive use of buyers and sellers.

A separate agora never materialized, but attempts were made to confine commercial activities to certain areas, mostly on the agora's open east side. Fishmongers, nut-sellers, honey-vendors, cobblers and others had their own districts, and each district took on the name of its specialty. Shoppers grew accustomed to describing their market-day itinerary in such terms as "I went off to the wine, the olive-oil and the pots," or "I went around to the garlic, and the onions, and the incense, and straight on to the perfume." Besides accommodating these districts within its ten-mile square, the agora also contained several small marketplaces. In the "women's agora" tunics, combs, waist-clinching girdles and other comforts and necessities were offered for sale by the women who produced them. In the Agora of Kerkopes, the original "den of thieves", the specialty was stolen goods.

The people coming in from the countryside and the itinerant pedlars sold most of their wares from the shaky, short-lived booths that were constructed along the open east side of the agora. Some goods were sold directly from the farmers' carts; some from hastily-erected tables. One sausage-seller carried his delectables about on a tray, setting it down wherever and whenever business was good. Another vendor marked his spot in the marketplace with a sunshade.

Most artisans and shopkeepers congregated in the cramped little rooms of a rambling set of buildings erected along the agora's north side. The rooms were constantly being overhauled and remodelled to accommodate new tenants. What had been a cookshop one month could easily become a carpenter's shop the next.

In the fifth century B.C. the citizens of Athens became preoccupied with adorning the agora with impressive public buildings that would be a credit to their new status as the acknowledged leaders of the Hellenic world. Providing a more orderly arrangement for the market people engaged the attention of a number of Athenians, most notably Xenophon, a man much concerned with the proper and efficient management of household and property. He advocated the construction of a special market building to house most of the buyers and sellers, one that would be not only a source of civic pride but also a source of substantial revenues.

A market building appeared in the fourth century, but it was not until the second century B.C. that the grand hall envisioned by Xenophon was built. The Stoa of Attalos was magnificent: two stories, marble facade, walls of Peiraeus stone, inner and outer columns, and terra-cotta roof.

Merchants willing to pay the high rents occupied the shops behind the colonnade. On the ground level was a spacious terrace where thriftier vendors sold their goods. Some market people completely ignored the new facilities and continued to sell from the familiar old booths and worn-down patches in the open square.

The arrangement for buying and selling in the Roman forum was similarly casual. Permanent commercial shops were tucked into public buildings. Flimsy stalls set up in an open square satisfied the simpler needs of farmers and pedlars. Cattle, pigs, fish, meat, vegetables and slaves were sold in special districts and separate markets within the forum. And there were always hucksters who managed to sell their goods in the middle of a jostling crowd.

All kinds and classes of people bought and sold in these ancient marketplaces. While a man of considerable means spent hours selecting one alabaster vial of sweet oil, his slave frantically searched the market for the best bargains, carrying an admonishment and complicated shopping list in his head: "Don't be extravagant, though not mean or stingy. . . . Some squids and cuttle fish, and should there be lobsters in the market, one should be fine, though two look well on the table. Now some eels come in from Thebes sometimes. Get some of them."[2] Many vendors in the market had nothing more in common than the fact that they had something to sell. A third-generation perfume-seller supervised the operation of his three shops in the market and "didn't know anything about debts", while not far away a cook, who had sold himself to the owner of an eating establishment in the agora, was always mindful of his debt as he waited on customers.

Despite the hodge-podge appearance of these markets in Athens and Rome they were well-regulated institutions. Both cities had huge populations to feed. By the fifth century B.C. a quarter of a million people lived in Athens and the surrounding territory. In the early days of the Roman Empire, several centuries later, Rome's population had climbed to a million. The markets had to be supervised and regulated to ensure that ample provisions were available and at a price peasants could afford. Grain, which both cities imported in enormous quantities, was the most closely supervised commodity in the markets. Each time it passed down the distribution chain—from grain merchant and importer to state official, to market commissioner, to baker's shop and finally into the hands of the citizens—it was inspected, weighed and tallied. Only in emergencies (such as famine and later inflation) was the price of grain fixed, though its distribution was always scrutinized to prevent speculation. But speculators appeared quite regularly anyway. When they were being especially efficient, bread riots would erupt. One Roman governor when visiting a provincial market noted that only cattle fodder was being offered for sale to the starving and angry crowds. When the people threatened to burn everything in sight, the governor denounced the grain merchants and plantation-owners for withholding the grain for export. His message to these speculators was clear: "The earth is the mother of us all, for she is just, but you in your injustice have acted as though she were your mother exclusively. If you do not stop, I will not let you exist upon her."[3] The speculators relented and flooded the market with grain.

Merchants, traders and shopkeepers conducted a large proportion of the trade in the markets in Athens and Rome. Though the officials recognized their role as essential when goods had to be carried over a long distance, middlemen were morally suspect. When Cicero distinguished between occupations that were dishonourable and those that were honourable and gentlemanly, he was especially hard on small-scale retailers and shopkeepers: "Those who buy from wholesalers for immediate resale are vulgar; their profits depend on misrepresentation, which is low and mean." Merchants, on the other hand, were the objects of a grudging respect: "Commerce on a small scale is vulgar, but if it is heavily capitalized, operates over a wide area, and benefits many people without misrepresentation, it is not much subject to criticism. If a merchant has a country estate to go to, it may even seem possible to justify praising him."

The Romans devised a series of laws to deal with the misrepresentation of goods in the marketplace, though the prevailing principle of sale was *caveat emptor*. It was up to the buyer to ensure that his purchase was not defective in any way. If the pomegranates he bought were old and bruised, he could do nothing. A buyer had the right to complain and force action only if the vendor had fraudulently concealed the flaws in his goods. In this case the seller was liable to the buyer for his loss. It was hard to misrepresent the quality of pomegranates but temptingly easy to hide the defects in commodities such as slaves and cattle. Special edicts covered their sale in which the seller guaranteed the soundness of his goods. If weaknesses turned up later, the buyer returned his purchase and recovered his cost.

The markets were notorious for their shady characters. Some sellers in the forum peddled goods to which they had no legitimate claim. Buyers could eventually lose their purchase if the original owners were lucky enough to track down their goods. Market laws in Rome made it possible for wary buyers to demand a promise from the vendor that if a challenger appeared with a better claim to the goods, the purchaser would be reimbursed.

Country people who traded in these markets seldom either bought or sold on a scale large enough to worry about these kinds of regulations. Their goods were inspected, weighed and sometimes taxed, like everyone else's. But compared to the high-stakes wheeling and dealing of the merchants, their

*This model of the Athenian agora shows a religious procession moving toward the Acropolis.*

routine was humble: "Often the farmer drove his sluggish donkey, loading its sides with oil or cheap apples, while on the return trip he brought back from town a grooved millstone or a lump of dark pitch."[5] Though their business was meagre, they were much more dependent on the agora or the forum than were the merchants. Merchants and shopkeepers could usually get on well enough without them; the city supplied all the buyers they needed. They could also pick up and take their goods elsewhere if necessary. But for the farmers these markets were the only places where they could convert their scant surplus into cash (or kind) and buy imported necessities such as salt and iron.

Outside the major centres of Athens and Rome and especially in areas that produced only one crop, local markets were even more crucial to the farmers' survival. Throughout the Roman Empire there were vast territories with too few people to support permanent market towns. Under these conditions periodic markets or fairs were set up once or twice a year at a village crossroads or on the estate of a big landowner. A village with several hundred people held a market more frequently. One small North African town included among its inhabitants "six ploughmen, four tenant-farmers, eight harvesters, two donkey-drovers, goat-herd, beet-seller, oyster-woman, cook, innkeeper, straw-seller, baker, linen-merchant, messenger, shopkeeper, bean-seller" and two market-women, or hucksters. In towns and villages like this, often two regular market days a month were scheduled. In larger towns there was usually a weekly market.

These rural markets attracted pedlars, merchants and farmers from miles around. Farmers and peasants set aside the whole day, travelling three or four hours very early in the morning with their donkeys loaded down with grain and chickens, figs and olives. By eight o'clock the market was already in full swing. After selling their goods the farmers,

with cash in their pockets perhaps for the first time that year, bought what they needed from the merchants' stalls and pedlars' sacks. The rest of the day they spent enjoying and refreshing themselves. Late in the evening they began their journey home, while pedlars tallied their profits and merchants packed up their goods for the trip to the next market or to the city, where they sold to the wholesalers what they had taken in trade from the farmers.

These markets operated in much the same way as those in the city. A market official supervised the transactions, inspecting goods and settling disputes. Weights and measures were checked to keep the dealing honest. Tolls were collected from buyers and from sellers. Merchants and pedlars who had travelled great distances were occasionally taxed for the privilege of selling in a local market.

Most merchants and pedlars travelling through the rural areas followed a circuit, moving from one market or fair to the next. The right to hold a market came directly from the state officials, from the Senate in Rome and later from the emperor. This kind of control was essential to ensure that the market days of neighbouring villages and towns would not conflict. Specific days were assigned when the right to establish a market was granted. To facilitate the movement of the merchants and pedlars one market would be held on Monday and another, perhaps twenty miles away, might operate on Wednesday or Thursday.

Market days were usually scheduled to coincide with public events and holidays, and most often with religious festivals. It was the easiest way of getting together a large concourse of buyers and sellers with an ample and varied stock of goods. It also guaranteed a good time. After worshipping at the shrine of Jupiter or Mercury, or following a day at the chariot-races, the festive crowds congregated at the merchants' stalls.

Roman market towns that were able to attract large

crowds of buyers and sellers prospered in more ways than the most obvious one—increased revenues from tolls and dues. Merchants who were drawn to the markets sometimes gave up their circuits to settle down and cater to the needs of one community. Tradesmen set up permanent shops to produce for one or perhaps two markets. Inns and stables were built to accommodate out-of-towners, taverns and eating establishments to refresh them, storerooms to hold their goods. Freemen flocked to these busy towns to work. Such good fortune was not common in most market towns. As well as a bustling marketplace, other factors—proximity to a major commercial centre, good roads, good land and good farmers—were important in deciding their destiny.

During the period of the Empire (31 B.C.—A.D. 476) new elements appeared that would seal the fate of some market towns. Maintaining the Empire was expensive. State officials began selling to a few enterprising businessmen the exclusive right to carry on certain trades and to sell certain commodities in the market. The state itself assumed the sole right to deal in some commodities by acquiring more and more of its citizens' produce as taxes. In the country the small-scale farmers were being forced off their subsistence plots and into the city slums by wealthy Romans who worked enormous areas of land with slave labour. Local commerce generally declined as the concentration of landholdings increased. And for the first time there were extensive controls in the markets. In A.D. 301 the Roman emperor published an edict that prescribed maximum prices for most goods, services and labour. It was an attempt to deal with inflation, and the emperor was careful to point out that avarice and gluttony were directly responsible for rising prices. Wheat was held at 100 *denarii* for a military peck; beef, mutton and goat, to 8 *denarii* per Italian pound (9¾ ounces); eggs, to 1 *denarii* each; soldiers' boots without nails, to 100 *denarii* per pair; a farm labourer's maximum

wage was set at 25 *denarii* a day with keep; an elementary teacher, 50 *denarii* per month per boy.

Many markets were not much affected by the trend toward monopolies and large landholdings. But in those towns and cities where both came together and joined hands with the state's price-setting program, the markets began to change. The kind of market in which no one person's interests prevailed, where a crowd of all kinds and classes of buyers and sellers competed more or less equally, was losing its foothold. The market would gradually evolve into one dominated by official control from the outside and privileged control from within.

Long before the Romans conquered Britain midway through the first century, their merchants had already established good trading relations with Celtic farmers in the south. Perhaps the merchants did some ranging through the countryside making private deals with the Celts, but more likely they either exchanged their pottery, wine and metal trinkets in the small markets occasionally set up in each hamlet or they organized their own markets or fairs. Around harvest time farmers from the surrounding countryside would assemble at a convenient time and spot prearranged by the merchants with sacks of surplus grain and with livestock they could not afford to feed over the winter.

The rules and customs of these markets were probably those the merchants had brought with them from their travels through the Empire. We have no idea how frequent these meetings were, nor how well organized. A safe conjecture is that, except for the faces of the buyers and sellers and some of their gestures, these markets and fairs were not much different than those in other small, rural communities in the Empire.

# 3 Markets in England in the Middle Ages

MOST markets in England through the early part of the Middle Ages were small and infrequent. Feudalism, which organized almost everyone's life from the eleventh to the thirteenth centuries, created a society that did not have much need for trade and exchange.

It was a society mostly of peasants who worked and lived on a manor. Within the manor village were the lord's house or a monastery, granaries and barns, a church, a marketplace, and a cluster of cottages where the tenants lived. Outside stretched three large open fields divided into narrow strips. Beyond the fields were the meadows for hay and beyond the meadows the common pasture for livestock.

Each peasant held some land. It was the same land and the same amount of land his family had held for generations. When a son inherited his father's holding, he also inherited his father's duties and obligations to the lord of the manor. The dues demanded for the privilege of farming sections of the lord's fields and grazing livestock in the lord's common pasture often included a cash rent, which never amounted to much because at the time money was not particularly useful or plentiful. More burdensome was the obligation to hand over to the lord's steward a portion of everything a family produced on its holding and in its household. The worst were the labour dues. Two or three days a month, more in the spring and fall, peasants worked their lord's farm, ploughing his fields, harvesting his grain, repairing his buildings and bridges, and carting his goods to market before their own.

Every year fifteen tenants at the Stevenage manor each paid about seventeen cents in cash, a bushel of wheat and sixteen eggs for their ten- to twenty-acre holdings. Each ploughed twelve acres, at the rate of an acre a day; harrowed four acres; reaped half an acre of wheat; harvested grain five halfdays a week until the job was done; carted two hundred pounds of wheat from Stevenage to Westminister (a twenty-mile, two-day journey) twenty times a year; and worked for the lord at whatever needed doing four halfdays every week. Most peasants paid a tax when they inherited their family holding (usually the best calf or ewe) and when their daughters married.

If all the peasants fulfilled their obligations, everyone on the manor was fed, clothed and sheltered—some better than others depending upon the degree of peasanthood they had inherited. Everything had its place, as in one great household. Each bushel of grain, each gallon of ale, each piece of cloth was produced and distributed according to the customs of the manor, which had been established generations before and very rarely changed.

To trade in the village market a peasant had to produce something that was not already spoken for in customary law. And there was seldom the energy and resources for that. The most he could hope for was having some wool left over, after paying his dues and clothing his family, to trade for salt to preserve a little meat for the winter. Peasants produced goods only for use in their own and their lord's households; nothing was produced specifically for the market. In the household economy that feudalism created, public markets were seldom anything but modest affairs.

England's market tradition comes more directly from the market towns that were created in the "golden era of borough-making", which reached its peak in the fourteenth century. By the fifteenth century about eight hundred market towns spread over the landscape of England and Wales. Life in these communities centred around the markets, and many of the five to seven hundred townspeople were either merchants who made their living selling from market stalls what they had bought at annual fairs, or craftsmen, artisans and trademen who produced goods specifically to sell for cash in the market.

The typical layout of these towns was either a long, single street with a marketplace in the centre or a junction of three roads with the market occupying the triangular spot where they met. In the marketplace the town's public buildings were constructed. Often there would only be the market hall with a room for a courthouse above, a jail below and shops at one end. Almost every town had a market cross. It was a many-sided building with an open archway on each side, the symbol of the town's market status and a reminder to everyone that fair and honest trading prevailed. Permanent shops, usually no more than small additions to the front of craftsmen's houses, were found in larger market towns.

Shambles were shakier structures constructed in the marketplace for the sale of meat and fish. Each town was required to have a common beam with standard weights and measures (usually very local measures) for hiring out to the vendors. Providing a pillory and a tumbrel, or cart, for punishing market offenders was another obligation set out in each town's market charter.

Acquiring market privileges from the king was one of the first steps in attaining town status. Late in the eleventh century William the Conqueror laid down laws that would govern the granting of market rights for most of the Middle Ages: "Let no market or fair be, or be permitted to arise, except . . . in very secure places where the customers of our kingdom and our common law and the dignities of our crown, which have been constituted by our good predecessors, cannot perish, or be defrauded or violated." At the same time William told his kingdom what a market ought to be like: "All things ought to be done regularly and openly and by judgment and justice."

Though most market towns appeared after William's conquest, they were bound by the same attitude that had prompted his prescription, which was that both buyer and seller were to benefit equally in any exchange of goods. The idea of a just price prevailed. One penny more and the seller was denounced and punished for self-interest and profit-making, since profit could only be made by taking advantage of his customers.

So the towns assembled all their buyers and sellers in one place at the same time to give full publicity and full supervision to the transactions. Every town had a company of officials charged with collecting tolls, inspecting private weights and measures and the quality of goods offered for sale. A small market town had four or five officials; in a town the size of Manchester forty officials supervised the market. There were toll-gatherers, sweepers, bellmen, ale-conners and bread-tasters, leather-searchers who inspected skins and hides, aulnagers who examined cloth, appraisers who assessed the value of goods, corn-lookers (or inspectors), fish-and-flesh lookers, and whitemeat lookers.

No matter how many officials each town elected or appointed, it was still hard to protect customers from being cheated. Private dealings outside the market and at any time other than during market hours—called forestalling—was strictly forbidden.

On market days a forestaller looking for gullible farmers stationed himself either at some strategic point along the road leading to town or just inside the door of an inn. Mentioning that he had just come from the market where the trade in grain was pitifully slow, he convinced farmers to sell their grain on the spot instead of hauling it all that way. When the forestaller took his cheaply-acquired grain to the market to sell, he committed his second market offense. Regrating or reselling goods at a higher price without adding any value to them (such as transporting them over a long distance) was also strictly forbidden, and regularly practiced. If the forestaller was especially daring, he would become an engrosser, hoarding vast quantities of grain and other goods until supplies diminished and prices rose. (In times of scarcity the just price went up. Just price was beginning to give way to market price, but no one admitted it.)

Engrossing was considered by far the most despicable crime of the three. A forestaller cheated one or two sellers; a regrater profited from one or two buyers. By controlling supplies and prices an engrosser took advantage of everyone. So everyone had the right to punish him. An engrosser spent hours with his head, hands and feet locked in the marketplace pillory, warding off insults and rotting vegetables.

On market days there was often one member of the victualling trades being either pilloried or dragged about on a tumbrel. They were usually bakers who sold underweight loaves or alewives who dispensed short measures and watered-down brew. During most of the Middle Ages the prices of the two staples of everyone's diet—bread and ale—were fixed at a regular meeting of the town officials, known as the assize. The only small coins in circulation were the penny, halfpenny and farthing, which meant that the assize could not alter the amount of money charged for bread and ale. Town officials fixed instead the weight of a loaf and the strength of ale.

Few customers bothered to weigh their loaves, which left them easy prey for unscrupulous bakers like John Brid. This fourteenth-century baker devised an ingenious scheme for squeezing a profit out of his unsuspecting customers. He cut an inconspicuous trapdoor in the table on which his customers set the dough they had brought to the market for him to bake. While he traded pleasantries with them, his apprentice stationed under the table "piecemeal and bit by bit craftily withdrew some of the dough", which was later formed into loaves and sold. Mr. Brid was eventually apprehended and dragged through the streets on a tumbrel with his underweight loaf dangling from a string around his neck. He might well have passed other tumbrels carrying bakers who had brought their loaves up to standard weight by inserting a piece of iron in the centre, or who had baked loaves with good dough on the outside and foul dough in the middle.

Bakers generally did a brisk business in any market. Only the wealthiest households included an oven; householders, finding the charred loaves that came out of the ashes of their open hearths barely edible, took their dough to the market each week and paid the baker to put it in the oven alongside his own loaves. Bakers also did a good trade in horse bread. Hay, which was seldom plentiful in the towns, was set aside for cattle; horses were fed a coarse dough of peas and beans.

In the summertime when grain supplies were running low, "what was detested by Dobbin was dealt to the hungry".

Next to the bakers, alewives were busiest on market day. They were required to put out a sign, leaves entwined around a pole, so that ale-testers could find them easily to test the strength of their ale and the size of their tankards before the market opened. Ale-testers discouraged alewives from tampering too much with the strength of their brew; to cheat their customers they resorted to lining the bottom of their tankards with dough, pitch or leaves. One alemonger named Alice was charged not only with selling her brew in quart tankards that were not really quarts but also with stuffing so much rosemary in the bottom of them that even six did not fill a gallon. Alice was not sentenced to the tumbrel; instead she spent a day in the *thewe*, or women's pillory.

After the bakers and alemongers, the most common occupants of the pillory and tumbrel were the butchers. Town officials supervised them closely to ensure that they sold meat that was "good and wholesome for a man's body". They could not sell by candlelight; their leftovers had to be salted; and they could not sell meat from animals that had died of unknown causes. However, they were often accused of selling "murrain cattle" and "putrid and stinking sheep".

Most markets had a cookshop crowded with hungry out-of-towners lining up for hot meat pies. Pastry could conceal the most unappetizing ingredients. The "putrefying eels" found in one cook's pies could at least be nosed out; the "garbage from capons, hens and geese" found in another's was harder to detect. Even more difficult for the market officials to expose were the cooks who used wholesome ingredients but befouled their culinary treats by handling them. Like the cook who made the pilgrimage to Canterbury:

> And he could roast and seethe and boil and fry
> Make good thick soup and bake a tasty pie.

> But what a pity—so it seemed to me
> That he should have an ulcer on his knee.[1]

Most of the people doing business in these markets were healthy and God-fearing. Very few of them in their lifetimes ever swindled a single customer or were so dim-witted as to be taken in by a forestaller. Though all transactions involved a lot of raucous haggling, almost everyone dealt honestly and peacefully. Swords, however, were banned in most marketplaces.

For their diligence in protecting buyers and sellers from the few exceptions, market officials were paid either in cash or kind, both of which were collected as tolls. Before the market bell was rung in the morning, corn-sellers opened their sacks for the toll-gatherer's dish. Most tolls were collected from buyers, at the rate of one penny a pig. Tolls were levied against out-of-town pedlars and merchants, and for the use of the common beam. Rent was collected from vendors if they were assigned a specific place in the market since that gave them the advantage of a permanent location. Neither the town nor its market officials ever got rich collecting tolls. They had to be a reasonable charge for services rendered and were usually fixed by customary law. Any tolls left over went toward civil and charitable projects: cleaning the town wells or buying bread for the poor.

Most towns grew and thrived because of their markets. The character of the countryside around them was changed too. With most town-dwellers busy manufacturing or preparing their goods for sale in the market, the job of feeding them fell to the farmers. They had an incentive to produce goods specifically for the market instead of only for household consumption. That meant cash, and with the cash they saved, those who were still bound to a feudal lord were able to buy off their labour obligations. Some eventually bought their freedom and moved to the country area surrounding London, which by the late Middle Ages had 50,000 people to feed.

London was one giant marketplace. Each of its dozen or so long-established markets spilled into the next one and filled the streets between. On the east side of the city going south from London Bridge was Leadenhall, where country people brought their butter and eggs and poultry to sell, mostly on the streets outside the great hall. Inside were the tradesmen selling leather and cloth and hardware.

Leadenhall's buyers and sellers joined up with the market people on Gracechurch Street. Across the foot of Gracechurch was the Eastcheap market where London's butchers assembled. Beyond Eastcheap was the New Fish Street market, home for the city's fishmongers. Along the east-west thoroughfare was the Cornhill market, next to it the Cheapside market, where every conceivable thing was sold from trestles, stalls and from open sacks on the ground: "meat, fish, poultry, tripe, trotters, pies, fruits, vegetables, cheese, butter, eggs, loaves, flowers, gingerbread, milk from the ass, bread for horses". Then Newgate Meal Market and finally the infamous St. Nicholas flesh shambles, where Samuel Pepys caused a riot one day when his coach upset a butcher's trestle.

Though London had a hundred times more mouths to feed and almost as many more buyers and sellers to worry about than the town markets, city officials vigorously and obstinately resisted altering any of the medieval traditions and customs of distributing food. Although drapers, mercers and most other craftsmen and merchants were retailing in permanent shops by the fifteenth century, private food dealing was still strictly forbidden. But no official resistance of any kind was strong enough to stop the changes that were coming.

At the end of the Middle Ages hundreds of hucksters were buying sacks of grain at one end of the market to sell in smaller quantities at the other. Food pedlars were doing well in the suburbs (suburban markets were not allowed until the seventeenth century), where residents "could ill-afford to take time off from their work to go to London's markets". Innkeepers were also surreptitiously selling food.

By the late sixteenth century Elizabethan London had 300,000 people. The traditional market, "principally intended for housekeepers buying on their own behoof", could not supply enough meat and grain to keep the city's brewers, bakers, butchers and cooks in business. Wholesalers, ignoring the time-honoured rules against forestalling, moved out into the country towns to buy up great quantities of livestock and grain to meet the needs of the city's victualling trades. They went off to the Leighton Buzzard market for cattle and to the towns in the Thomas Valley for barley and wheat. Small-town millers grew rich grinding meal for London bakers. By the early seventeenth century the network of dealers and their appreciative customers had become too powerful to fight. In 1684 London officials were forced to abandon their medieval attitudes about how food ought to be distributed and to allow wholesale markets in the city.

Other changes came much more slowly. Until the end of the nineteenth century most housekeepers were still making weekly trips to the market to buy fresh provisions directly from the country people. Up to the 1870s the grocers' stock-in-trade included tea, coffee, cocoa, pepper, salt, spices and scent. Greengrocers with fresh fruits and vegetables, butter, eggs, cheese and bacon were hard to find in London and almost impossible to find outside the city. But when the change came it was dramatic.

In the second half of the nineteenth century the number of consumers doubled and the standard of living rose sharply. Enterprising businessmen, with not a single medieval notion left in their heads, eagerly went after these new consumers, operating not one but many retail food shops and selling not just nonperishable items but fresh provisions as well. Thomas Lipton opened his one-man grocery shop in Glasgow in 1872; in 1890 he was operating seventy Lipton's Markets in London; by 1898 there were 285 of them spread throughout Britain.

Though complaints were rare (because alternatives were), shopping for groceries in a market was a battle of elbows and wits. Housekeepers faced short-tempered, noisy crowds, quarrelsome butchers and disagreeable egg-sellers, rain or shine. They guessed at weights, worried about swindlers, paid cash and carted home, unaided, baskets spilling over with turnips, cheese and unwrapped loaves and sausages. In the grocer's shop everything was orderly and serene. Customers were waited on, with pleasure, by upstanding shopkeepers in bright white coats. Credit was extended and groceries delivered.

In the public market, though customers' interests were diligently safeguarded, sellers always had the upper hand. In the grocers' shops the buyer was finally becoming king.

# The Market Tradition in Canada

EARLY settlers in Canada had all they could do just managing to wrest from their new land enough food to keep their families from starving. Potatoes, a small patch of grain, a garden plot, one or two pigs, a milk cow and a few chickens kept these families from perishing in their first years as pioneers. Everywhere they were engaged in subsistence farming and had nothing to spare. And for most of them it would be many years before they had anything to trade with their neighbours in a market.

The first trading these pioneers did was with merchants and shopkeepers in the nearest village or town. Most settlers were dependent on shopkeepers almost from the day they arrived to take up their land. At the store they were outfitted with everything they needed—enough flour, sugar, salt and other groceries to get them at least through the first season; tools, often livestock, seed for grain and vegetables, and if they could afford it, a plough.

The whole country started off on shopkeepers' credit. Farmers opened accounts and promised to pay for everything when the first harvest was in. The experience of one settler in the West was a common one for pioneers everywhere in Canada:

It was hard times those years. You only had money in the fall when you could sell something. Nobody had much money and we had none. I was living with my brother at the time because I hadn't built my house yet. We went to town, oh, about 25 miles, this spring day and we had orders from his wife for 60 dollars' worth of groceries.

When we got there they refused us . . . credit. There were two stores there, Snyder and Armstrong, and a store down the street. They'd give credit to others, but they wouldn't to me and my brother. I hadn't a crop yet, but he had and he'd of paid them in the fall.

When we couldn't get credit at Snyder, we said we'd try the other store. We went down there and they knew we'd been getting our groceries at Snyder's and paying cash for it so they said, "No, you been getting your groceries up the street, so you can go get your credit there."

We both had families, babies had been born, and we couldn't go home without anything and have our children starve, so we went back to Snyder and Armstrong and they said, "Did you get it?" And we said no. They sort of smiled at us.

I didn't say this but my brother did and he said, "By God, we're not going home without them groceries. We're gonna bust in to get it. We'll wait around and then we'll bust into your damn store tonight and we'll get it, and I don't mean maybe. We got kids out there and we need 60 dollars' worth of groceries and if you don't want to sell them to us in an honest way, then we're gonna steal 'em tonight. And I'm telling you I'm not kidding you." He was mad.

The storekeeper said, "Give me the list," and my brother give it to him and he handed it to his helper and he said, "Fill it out." That's all he said. In fact, when the final reckoning come that bill was worth about 70 dollars. About 10 dollars more.[1]

Snyder and Armstrong seemed unusually cantankerous for pioneer shopkeepers. It was rarely that difficult for settlers to get credit, but it was always that crucial. When starvation was the only alternative, theft did not seem entirely unreasonable.

In the beginning merchants and shopkeepers handled most of the food trade. They imported necessities that the community could not produce; they took the farmers' grain, potatoes, eggs, butter and meat in exchange for store merchandise; and they sold the country produce to town customers and to merchant-wholesalers who had sold them their own stock on credit.

The first markets in Canada appeared in garrison and government towns, such as Halifax and Toronto, where there were many soldiers and civil servants to feed. A steady demand for the products of their farms encouraged country people to improve their agricultural skills, raise better livestock, and cultivate their fields more carefully. Farm women and children spent longer hours in their gardens, in their poultry yards and at the butter churn. What had not been promised to storekeepers was sold in the markets.

Towns in the Maritimes and in Upper and Lower Canada that had no garrisons established markets when their populations reached about five hundred and when the surrounding countryside was supporting enough farmers able to produce a surplus. At first little was sold in these markets. For at least the first half of the nineteenth century townspeople kept a cow in the backyard along with a few chickens; they grazed a few sheep and sometimes cattle in the town's common pasture, and they left their pigs to wander the streets in search of whatever nourishment they could find. In the market they bought mostly meat and vegetables from farmers and bushels of turnips to feed their livestock in the winter.

When these towns prospered, so did their markets. In most cases they flourished in the mid-nineteenth century when populations had climbed and most town and city dwellers were engaged in commercial and industrial activities. Markets multiplied and specialized. In most towns there were separate hay, cattle and wood markets, besides the main market where butchers sold their carcasses of beef and farmers their vegetables, butter and eggs. Farmers were still selling most of their grain to merchants, but they were also producing goods specifically for sale in the markets. There they could sell for cash, and often it was the only cash they received. Many of them were still bound by credit to merchants.

The rules that regulated these markets were, with few exceptions, the same rules that governed markets in Europe

in the late Middle Ages. Markets in early Canada were established, as they had been for thousands of years elsewhere, for the benefit of the whole community. To ensure that the country people carting their produce to town on market day had customers waiting for them, storekeepers and butchers in most towns and cities were obliged to close down their shops while the market was open. Customers were protected by diligent officials who searched the market for unwholesome food. Public weigh scales were set up outside most market houses, and vendors were charged a nominal toll for using them.

Every town had a market square and held its first market in the open air. Later the market moved inside to share quarters with the town council, the post office, the jail and the library. Those were the days when there was only one public building in town. The space reserved for the market doubled as a political arena, a wrestling ring, a dance-hall and sometimes a courtroom. Shambles, or sheds, to house the town's butchers and farmers selling meat were the first buildings to go up on market square. They were thrown together as quickly and cheaply as possible and usually did not stand solid for long. But for a few years they kept the beef and pork out of the sun and rain and away from the dust, mud and traffic on the streets.

The first real market house built in most towns put the townspeople heavily in debt. But when the size of the debt was measured against the need to accommodate more vendors and the greater need to provide more sanitary surroundings, the people voted eventually for a new market house. Most were modest, functional, long rectangular buildings, with butchers' stalls down one side and tables set up for the country people along the other side and down the centre aisle of the hall.

After a town had enjoyed a few years of prosperity, had incorporated as a city and had joined Confederation,

prominent citizens began agitating for a new city hall and a new market hall. This time modesty and functionalism were not primary considerations; the new market building was to be a civic ornament. What these citizens wanted above all was something that would gratify their civic pride. The expense would be considerable, so a great deal of long-winded effort was required to recruit sympathizers and convince the others.

In 1851 when Joseph Howe, editor of the *Novascotian*, learned that many prominent people in Halifax were opposed to erecting a new market house, he took up the issue with his readers: "Nothing is better established than the fact that the new market house will pay its own expense and that the citizens will not be taxed to make good any deficiencies. . . . We are at a loss to know why any person should kick against the proposed improvement on the eve of its consummation." The next time he attempted to persuade his readers, having been unsuccessful the first time, he tried to shame them into agreeing to spend the money to replace the "most disgraceful Shanty"—the Halifax Market Hall: "We recommend that a glass case be at once procurred and the building in question be enclosed for exhibition at the World Fair in London. It would be an apt illustration of the utter want of public spirit which characterizes a rising City with a population of 25,000 souls." Three years later Mr. Howe got his fine new market house.

Unfortunately, the new Halifax market house, like most of the others that civic pride built in the last half of the nineteenth century, was underused as a market. Cities were optimistic about everything then and erected market houses large enough to accommodate almost twice as many vendors as the old ones. The rationale was that if the market house were larger, more country people would want to rent stalls, and that if it were more lavishly outfitted, more city people would be lured to its doors. The presumption was that

everything else would stay the same. But not long after these great market halls were built—many of them with promenades; some outfitted as concert halls; Victoria's embellished by two ornamental fountains—business in most markets began to decline.

In 1888, less than a decade after Saint John's "handsome and commodious" market house had opened, a writer for the *Sun* noticed a dramatic change in the food trade and what effect it would have on the city market:

> For some years after it was erected the country market was the centre to which came the great bulk of the fruits of the earth from a large range of country, but the opening up of new lines of railway, and the development of the steamboat accommodation on the St. John River, Grand Lake, Washademoak, etc., have had the effect of turning much of the former supply into other channels. There is a marked yearly increase in the volume of agricultural products that reaches St. John—the supply keeping pace with the ever enlarging demand—but a large portion thereof is caught up at Indiantown and on the outskirts of the city by enterprising traders and commission merchants. Indeed, the commission business has of late years developed wonderful proportions. Then, again, enterprising merchants, pushing their buyers out into the country, buy direct from the farmers and country storekeepers, who in their turn gather up all marketable material in their several localities, sending it not to the country market, but to St. John commission merchants. The current of trade from the upper St. John district has changed, and much of the surplus produce of that region now finds its way by rail to the United States. What does come now . . . to St. John . . . is almost altogether handled by large commission men and wholesale dealers.
>
> All these causes combine to materially affect the trade done in the country market and reduce the revenue derived from tolls. . . .

The same thing was happening almost everywhere in

Canada, sooner in some communities than in others. The railway, steamship and improved roads opened up much larger, and more intangible, markets for farmers. Selling in bulk at the farm gate was easier than selling in the market. Farmers started specializing to give the wholesalers more of what they wanted.

Grocers in their neat and tidy shops were drawing customers away from the market. They offered variety, credit and home delivery, and eventually canned goods. Also, the market was a sign of the city's past, and citizens were feeling progressive. So they deserted their market with a clear conscience.

In the early years of the twentieth century the decline in market revenues was becoming noticeable but was not yet alarming. Business picked up during the First World War, held on through the Depression and accelerated again during the Second World War. After that most markets went into a steady decline.

In the 1950s, sometimes earlier, most markets were no longer supporting themselves. They had lost so many vendors (and customers) that rents from stalls failed to cover the costs of operating them. Some cities were spending as much as ten thousand dollars a year to keep their markets open. City officials were seldom exacting in the repair and maintenance of the buildings, mainly because they could not afford to be. The market houses of which citizens had once been so proud deteriorated into dilapidated white elephants. One solution most cities tried was leasing out part of these buildings as bowling alleys, bus terminals, railway stations or lost animal shelters.

Almost all market halls built in the nineteenth century were situated on valuable city property. In the 1960s when officials decided to give their cities a facelift and a commercial boost, the market halls were among the first buildings to go. In their places rose a shopping centre in Halifax, a cultural centre in Charlottetown, a shopping complex in Kitchener and a parking lot in Regina.

Markets came later to the West, but by the 1950s and '60s they had developed a similar pattern to those in the East. Market halls disappeared everywhere in Canada at about the same time. Because markets had a shorter life in the West and producers and consumers had developed other buying and selling habits before the markets were established, the market tradition was never as strong there as in the East.

In the 1970s the provincial governments of Alberta and Saskatchewan initiated programs to encourage communities to set up local farmers' markets. Both governments wanted to encourage producers and consumers to meet face-to-face; to give small-scale farmers an outlet for their goods; to increase the production of fruits and vegetables; and to provide some stiff competition for chain-store supermarkets. In cities and small communities in both provinces, farmers' markets are being created, operated and patronized with great enthusiasm. In the late 1970s British Columbia was considering setting up its own farmers' market program.

While the market tradition is being rediscovered in the West, it is stronger now in the East than it has been for forty years and often much longer. The market people there, especially those whose families have been customers and vendors for three or four generations, have kept their tradition alive.

# 4 Charlottetown Farmers' Market

CHARLOTTETOWN built four market houses within a hundred years, and each one was larger and more handsome than the last. The market house expanded with the town, taking on a grander proportion and style as the face and nature of Charlottetown and its countryside changed.

Early in 1807 Samuel May Williams was commissioned by Lieutenant Governor DesBarres to build Charlottetown's first market house. It was a plain rectangular frame structure with a loft above the ground floor. When it opened it was barely large enough to hold a dozen farmers bartering their grain and underfed livestock. But as small and homely as the first market house was, it was all the community needed.

Early in the nineteenth century, after years of political calamity, Charlottetown and its countryside were just beginning to acquire the features of permanent and civilized settlement. To the visitor it looked like a composed and orderly little town. The Charlottetown settlement occupied seventy-three hundred sparsely populated acres. There were almost seventy unpainted frame houses scattered along the wide streets. Three public buildings shared the large open square in the middle of the town—the new market house, the combined courthouse and legislative chamber and the log jailhouse. There was one church, a few shops selling imported dry goods, tea, sugar, molasses and tobacco, and an inn running a healthy business in rum and brandy. Down by the wharves stood Benjamin Chappell's post office.

To the townspeople Charlottetown was still a pioneer settlement. At the first sign of rain the streets turned into "mud holes, hog wallows and filth-carrying gutters". The two roads which connected the town with villages on Malapeque and St. Peter's bays were nothing more than worn paths. The times still required that everyone be something of a farmer. Most of the families acquired town lots adjacent to their homes for growing a basic supply of vegetables and fruit. Every family pastured a cow, a few sheep and perhaps a horse on the twelve-acre lot located on the outskirts of town. Extending beyond the pasture was a five-hundred-acre common where Charlottetowners cut endless cords of firewood.

The Loyalist, Scottish and English immigrants who farmed the countryside were still engaged in pioneer agriculture. They laboured through the early spring and late fall to convert the dense bush into farmland. In the already cleared but still stumpy fields stood patches of potatoes, wheat, barley, oats and timothy, with a few scattered plantings of

Facing p. 31: *Charlottetown's fourth market house.* Opposite: *Butchers' stalls in Charlottetown's fourth market house.* Left: *Charlottetown's Round Market House.*

flax and turnips. A few fortunate farmers had a single-furrow plough outfitted with a broad share for manoeuvring around stumps, but for most of them farming had not progressed beyond sickles, spades and hoes. Grain was broadcast by hand, cut with scythes, gathered with wooden rakes and threshed with flails. Potatoes were dropped into shallow furrows, covered with manure and harvested by hand. For most of the year, especially after the hay supply had been exhausted in mid-winter, the cows, oxen and swine were left to scavenge for food in the partly-cleared bush.

Contemporary assessments of the likelihood that these farmers would survive, let alone succeed, were hardly encouraging. One early visitor reduced the entire Island to "a rascally heap of sand, rock and swamp . . . a lump of worthlessness that bears nothing but potatoes". Another reported that "the general mode of conducting a Farm was slovenly, often wretched".

If Charlottetowners noticed the wretched and slovenly agricultural skills of the farmers, they did not seem to mind. They regularly gathered in the market house to buy hay and flour, potatoes and mutton, stalks of domestic currants, flower seeds and gooseberries, raw wool and kegs of butter. And they exchanged news. About Thomas Cummins, for

instance, who had been sentenced to thirty-nine lashes in front of the jail, thirty-nine more opposite the stocks and another thirty-nine in front of the market house, on three consecutive days, for stealing a pig. Or about another tenant farmer who had defaulted on his rent and feared eviction by his British landlord.

When the second market house opened on Queen Square in 1823, Charlottetown's rough frontier features were being transformed into those of a prospering colonial town, and its citizens were turning from part-time farmers to full-time consumers. Town lots were filling up with merchants, shipbuilders, land agents and tradesmen too preoccupied with building and running their town to worry about feeding themselves. New shops were advertising imported shingles and covered furniture, the latest bonnets and dressmaking to order. An amateur theatre was starting a two-season run of English farce and melodrama. The town was beginning to enjoy life.

The new market house was an eccentric and fanciful sixteen-sided building. Round Market House had a window in each of its sixteen walls; its exterior was surrounded by a seven-foot-wide colonnade outfitted with sixteen pillars that supported an overhanging cupola-crowned roof. Double doors opened onto Queen Square where farmers parked their hay and straw carts.

More farmers from the countryside were making the twice-weekly trip to market to benefit from the new crop of consumers. But as the trade in produce and livestock increased, so did the temptation to scrimp on weights and measures. To ensure that when a customer paid for ten pounds of mutton she was getting ten true pounds, a large set of public scales was set up along the west side of the market house. Above the scales hung a warning from Proverbs: "A false measure is an abomination to the Lord, a just weight is His delight."

By the time Charlottetown was incorporated as a city in 1855, sterner measures for protecting consumers were required. One of the new city council's first items of business was devising regulations for "the good government of Market House". The council, at its long-winded best, ordered that hereafter

> should any diseased, unwholesome or unsound meat of any description or measly pork be exposed for sale, the Market Clerk shall forthwith seize and shall cause the person exposing such meat or pork to be summoned before the Mayor's or Police Court, which said court shall have the power to cause same to be publicly burnt if after hearing evidence it shall consider such meat or pork as unfit for food and may further enforce a fine not exceeding forty shillings on the person or persons who may have exposed the same for sale and enforce payment of same by distress of imprisonment of the offender for a term not exceeding thirty days, unless the said fine be sooner paid.[1]

To further protect citizens, this time from their own weak wills, the council soon changed market days from Wednesday and Saturday to Tuesday, Thursday and Friday "to help a more perfect observance of the Sabbath" and "a diminution of drunkenness".

Not long after Charlottetown's incorporation, when the heyday of Round Market House was well past, citizens began to grumble about "that miserable little edifice, which nearly half a century ago was erected among the stumps on Queen Square, and which is now only fit for a bonfire". They wanted a new market house "that would be a credit to the city". There was considerable discussion about the location of the new market. At least one Charlottetowner strongly objected to erecting it on the same site on Queen Square, right next to the gracious and dignified Colonial Building, because of "the presence there on market days of many animals with resulting manure, a litter of loose hay and straw, fish, lobster shells and other objectionable matter being strewn about the Square". Most Charlottetowners argued for retaining the original site. The House of Assembly was petitioned by "divers inhabitants and owners of real estate" not to sanction "in any way or under any pretext, any measure calculated to have the effect of establishing a Public Market for Charlottetown on any site other than the Queen Square, as its location and direct connection with the principal streets of the City and roads leading there to make it a superior location".[1] They won the battle, and in 1867 Charlottetowners got an enormous and imposing two-story brick market house in the centre of Queen Square.

These were heady years for Charlottetown. The city deserved its grand and handsome new market house. From a busy colonial town it had become a proud provincial capital and important commercial centre. Its wharves were crammed in the fall with steamships loading cargoes of oats, potatoes and squared timber bound for the American states, Miramichi, Halifax, England and Ireland.

In the last half of the nineteenth century the countryside was seeing good times as well. Farming literature from England had found its way to the Island. Judge Peters's *Practical Hints to the Farmers of Prince Edward Island*, a

distillation of Jethro Tull's *The Horse-Hoeing Husbandry* with an original and imaginative treatise on manuring, and the writings of Halifax's Agricola were making converts to "high-farming". The Charlottetown Farmers' Society was introducing better breeds of livestock. Ayrshire and Shorthorn cattle were replacing the stunted Acadian breeds; Lincoln and Hampshire sheep were taking over from the long-legged, white-faced and casually bred stock; and Yorkshire and Berkshire swine were edging out the breed that an early visitor had described as "looking like greyhounds nearly as much as they do the better kind of Hogs". Farms in the Charlottetown countryside were nearly all cleared. Fields were being worked with a two-furrow plough drawn by a team of draft horses; grain was being threshed and fanned instead of stooked and flailed. Farmers were acquiring the skills and knowledge to supply a year-round market.

On market days the market house was full of squawking hens, running children, shouting vendors and arguing shoppers. It was still the best place for passing on news and gossip and for celebrating civic occasions and complaining publicly about injustices. When Charlottetown threw a party for the new queen Victoria, the community, abundantly refreshed and entertained at the city's expense, danced and caroused in market square all day and night.

In 1902 a raging winter fire destroyed Charlottetown's third market house. The fourth market house, which Mayor Warburton promised would be "an ornament to the city", took almost two years to build. In the meantime farmers and Charlottetowners met in a shabby little frame building called Market Shack. The new building was another very large two-story brick structure with room for a hundred butchers and vendors.

For the next three decades buying and selling in the market on Queen Square continued as it had for the previous fifty years, with everyone in the community turning out every market day. But shortly after the Second World War there were clear signs of change. For the first time many empty stalls appeared in the market as more and more farmers were beginning to sell to wholesalers supplying grocers and the export trade. A large gathering hall and offices were rented out on the top floor, and the basement was converted into a bowling alley and eventually a bus terminal. In 1949 Edwin Johnstone, Chairman of the Market Committee, reported that "it is questionable whether the services being rendered to the community by the market justify the high costs of its maintenance". Market expenses continued to outrun revenue from tolls and rents. Its end was already in sight when the city began making plans to build a cultural centre on the Queen Square market site.

Before the wrecker's ball touched it, the market house burned to the ground. Some Islanders considered the fire a convenient turn of events; others more cynical about the need for a monolithic and expensive cultural centre thought the fire was a little too convenient, and that the city's storekeepers would be the last citizens to mourn the end of competition from the market. In 1958, in his annual report to the citizens of Charlottetown, Mayor Edwin Johnstone lamented the city's misfortune but went on immediately with plans to replace the market house: "In April last Charlottetown and indeed the province as a whole suffered a severe loss through the complete destruction by fire of our market building, but already plans are afoot for a modern Civic Centre to replace that building, and this Council has taken steps which may well lead to the same becoming a reality in the near future." Confederation Centre for the Arts now stands on the old market site on Queen Square.

For the next eighteen years there was no market in Charlottetown. In 1976 a few Queen's County farmers began a quiet campaign to re-establish it. Disheartened by the

outrageous prices being charged in local supermarkets, Charlottetowners would support a farmers' market, they hoped. But it was not easy attracting consumers back to the market. The older citizens had lost the habit of buying in a market, and younger ones had never acquired the skills to banter and bargain for their week's groceries.

By May a half-dozen small-scale farmers and large-scale gardeners had been coaxed into loading their trucks with lettuce, radishes, spinach and peas and setting up their own market in the parking lot behind the downtown Eaton's store. The first summer the market was a curiosity. An afternoon spent shopping for shorts and shoes now included a stroll through the truck market. But as casual as the market was, vendors were satisfied with their returns. By the end of the summer a truckload of fresh vegetables was fetching a few hundred dollars in cash every Saturday morning. The next summer the Island's Market Development Corporation paid for the cost of constructing tables for the market and shared the cost of advertising with the vendors.

When the market later moved to permanent quarters in the Farm Centre on University Avenue, the market lost many of its loyal downtown customers. Its new customers were young suburban families ill-at-ease with the ways of the public market. They were shy asking prices and enquiring about what was to be done with the strange bags of middlings. But by the time they had made their way through the market, they were placing orders for the next market day. And as they left they were directing newcomers to the rapidly diminishing supply of bannock and bran muffins.

The Charlottetown Farmers' Market is small, modest and at times surprisingly sedate. But the signs of a good market are there. Shoppers pause over their purchases and vendors are easily engaged. A charming, long-skirted schoolteacher from a nearby Belfast farm each week fills a dairycase full of her own butter, cottage cheese, yogurt and sour cream, and

spreads a small table with sheepskin booties, bullhide moccasins and round, heavy loaves of bannock. At another table a housewife and her young daughters sell jams, jellies, pies, eggs and gooey-rich squares. At the head table a demure Highlander fidgets with her careful display of needlework while her urbane, potato-inspector husband watches over the beets, pumpkins, gourds and bars of New Brunswick maple cream. Next a bashful young farmer with sacks of new potatoes and freshly dug carrots. Finally a cheeky old shorthorn breeder from Mount Herbert who gruffly explains to everyone who asks about the milling process that produced his flour, shorts, germ and middlings. To this refreshingly forthright gentleman, who would never admit how much he enjoys the market, Charlottetowners owe a good part of their gratitude for the revival of their market tradition.

# 5 Halifax City Market

WHEN travellers in the nineteenth century wanted to get a good idea of what a colonial town or city was like, they visited its market. Just before mid-century the Halifax market was carefully scrutinized by at least two visitors, one a famous English writer, the other a slightly abrasive Yankee pedlar. On their respective visits Charles Dickens and Sam Slick gathered quite different impressions of both the town and its market.[1]

Joseph Howe escorted Charles Dickens to Province House, ("a gem of Georgian architecture") to the opening of the provincial legislature ("looking at Westminster through the wrong end of a telescope") and to the market at Cheapside. Dickens wrote later that the market was "abundantly supplied and exceedingly cheap", just what one would expect in a "cheerful, thriving and industrious" town.

Sam Slick probably visited the market alone, and probably tried to peddle some clocks while he was there. He could not have been very successful. The markets were "so confoundedly dull," Slick told a travelling companion. He did not think much better of the town: "Halifax reminds me of a Russian officer I once seed at Warsaw; he had lost both arms in battle." Or the people: "The strange critters, they are all asleep. They walk in their sleep, and talk in their sleep, and what they say one day they forget the next; they say they were dreamin'."

Perhaps their different impressions of the market resulted from Dickens approaching it as a buyer and Slick as a seller. An "abundantly supplied and exceeding cheap" market meant a confoundedly slow and unprofitable one for vendors. Though Dickens's impressions of a thriving people did not come from the market, the country vendors probably took care to appear cheerful and industrious in order to attract customers. Leaving aside the armless Russian officer, Sam Slick probably found his "strange critters" in the market as well, and more than likely they were his customers.

The market these gentlemen were describing was sprawled out on the streets and sidewalks adjoining market square. While the town's butchers occupied the market house built for them in 1807, the country people peddled their eggs, butter and produce by the cartload in the open air. For years they had ignored the little market shanty that Halifax had put up for their use across from the butchers' shambles.

When a large stone and brick market house was constructed in the 1850s with room for fifty vendors, they ignored it too and continued to sell where they had always sold, on the streets and sidewalks close to Market Slip.

Within the next decade Halifax was famous up and down the Atlantic coast for its colourful, crowded street market. Visitors from as far away as New York had heard about it, probably from Haligonians who eagerly publicized its "rustic charm".

A highly picturesque feature of Halifax has always been the "Green Market" held on Wednesday and Saturday mornings on the sidewalks near the post office and Market Slip. All summer through, as regularly as these mornings come, came a mixed company of "Chezzetcookers" and Negroes, the former some of the dark-skinned descendants of the Old Acadians who have been accustomed to troop into town across the Dartmouth Ferry, their rude wagons laden with farm produce, poultry, flowers and small domestic wares of various sorts and ranging themselves along the sidewalks unobtrusively offering their goods for sale.[2]

The merchants in the town found the country vendors neither unobtrusive nor colourful. In their softer moments the shopkeepers called the country people obstinate and bothersome. "Every Wednesday and Saturday hay carts were ranged along the curb stones on Bedford Row from Walsh's Corner to Lithgow's building, blocking the traffic and leaving litter," a spokesman for the merchants complained. "It was unfair to the merchants who paid heavy taxes and who had built a row of houses that were an ornament to the City."

The city fathers knew better than to ignore the grumblings of the merchants. One alderman went so far as to propose that "no person be allowed to sell vegetables outside the city market while the stalls inside are unoccupied, and when owing to the crowded state of the market, persons cannot obtain a place to offer their goods for sale they shall be allowed to use the space outside by paying the same fee as the occupants of the stalls inside". With a little more diplomacy the mayor added that "besides it is pitiful on stormy days to see so many country people exposed to the rain and tempest without shelter of any kind".

Neither threat nor tempest worried the country vendors. Throughout the nineteenth century they continued to hold their market where they wanted to hold it—close to Market Slip. The distance from the Slip was one of their complaints

Opposite: *Scenes from the LaPierre farm, c.1905.* Below: *The Green Market, c.1906.*

about the new market house. Another was the fact that the city butchers occupied all the best stalls in the market. At least one of their customers complained to the city fathers about the meat-sellers' clique. "We cannot understand why the building which was assigned for a Green Market should be occupied almost wholly by resident butchers. The butchers possess a great deal of wealth and are quite able to put up buildings of their own."

There were stronger sentiments behind the country vendors' stubborn resistance to the market house. Its stalls were rented for an annual sum of two pounds, which was a lot more than most of them were willing to pay. And they were a conservative group. Their families had been selling in the open air for generations. Until they were forced to change they would hold on to their traditional ways.

At the turn of the century the city fathers thought it was time Halifax got itself a market as grand as the one in Saint John. When they opened their new building in 1916, they were not taking any chances with the country people. Twelve police officers were assigned to meet the Dartmouth Ferry and escort the vendors to the new market on Brunswick Street. "Quite a few country people were inclined not to heed their direction and took up positions around the usual square on Hollis Street and Bedford Row. The officers, however, finally persuaded those to leave and most found their way to the new market."

Though the country vendors went to the new market house, probably more out of curiosity than anything, they did not go quietly. The city fathers offered free refreshments and two weeks free rent, but nothing would stifle the vendors' disgruntlement. The city fathers could make them use the new market, but they could not force them to like it. "It was alright but for the getting here," one of them breathlessly exclaimed after cajoling his team to the site in the shadow of Citadel Hill. Another thought the building sufficient but the rental fees outrageous. They would gobble up the small profit he was eking out of the market now. Another group claimed that the market facilities were inadequate. "When the new vegetables are in their plenty the building would not hold near half of the goods. Again there was not sufficient stalls for the horses."

The new market house turned out to be not so bad after all. Though the country vendors never really warmed to the idea of selling inside the market house, they quickly grew accustomed to its comforts. It shaded them from the hot summer sun and sheltered them from rain and snowstorms. It also seemed to help business. There were more shoppers in the market than on the streets, and selling became more competitive when it moved inside. The best vendors were the best showmen. Their more reticent neighbours in the market fought back whenever they could by cutting their prices by a cent or two.

Selling in the market was good for everybody for most of the first few decades of the twentieth century. During the war years as many as 175 vendors sold their goods in the market. With all this healthy activity the building started to crumble in the corners. It was, in fact, the mayor admitted, "slowly falling to pieces". By the late 1940s some of the city fathers were suggesting that doing away with the market house—and perhaps even the market—was worth serious consideration.

The provincial government stepped in to cut short such reveries. Pointing to an 1815 bylaw and the city's original charter it declared that the city had an obligation to house the market people somewhere. Chagrined and stumped by the provincial edict, city council dropped the issue for a while. The market house continued to crumble.

A few years later the need for massive renovation was inescapable, when shoppers found it almost too hazardous to pause over a bushel of apples. Two floors were added and the mouldering corners repaired. The city police moved in upstairs. But the market was still to face its biggest problem. The market house was downtown, right in the centre of a maze of narrow, winding streets that had seemed reasonable when General Cornwallis laid them out in 1749, but made no sense at all to shoppers trying to park their cars just long enough to dash through the market.

The vendors had no hope of attracting new customers and only a faint hope of holding on to their regulars. The number of shoppers declined and so did the number of vendors. In the 1960s not even half the number of vendors who had rented space during the war years were now bothering to come to the market. Though parking was the worst problem, it was not the only one. The market house was cold and drafty in the winter, and there were no washrooms.

In 1969 the decaying old market building was demolished to make way for Scotia Square. The country people were promised better accommodation elsewhere. Experience should have taught them to be wary. They have not had a permanent market location since then.

For the next few years room was made for them in the basement of the Industrial Building in the city's Forum Complex. The number of vendors selling regularly again fell by half. Parking was no longer a problem, but almost everything else was. But the thirty-odd vendors persevered more for principle than for profit.

They lost that spot within five years and set up their tables in the Civic Arena. The dozen or so vendors remaining now interfered with skating, so they were moved upstairs to the corridors surrounding the arena floor. It was a dingy spot that smelled like a locker room. But as grotty as it was, it was better than the parking lot outside on a cold October morning, which was where they were directed when the city's custodians went on strike. The market has become a game of hide-and-seek, with the vendors having no more idea than the customers where they will be hiding next.

The only thing that has not changed is the country vendors. They are still obstinate, still feisty and still coming in every market day from the same areas vendors have been coming from since the market opened 250 years ago. The country people who charmed Charles Dickens with their cheerful faces and industrious hands have descendants still selling regularly in the market.

The bashful lady selling her maple-splint baskets belongs to a Cherry Brook family that has been making baskets for six generations and selling them in the Halifax market for four. The Cheapside market near the ferry wharf was the only place in the beginning where the black community could sell anything. In the spring there were bunches of mayflowers, pussy willows, clumps of ferns, peas and bean poles to sell; in the wintertime Christmas wreaths, holly and garlands of evergreens. It was almost forty years ago that this woman learned to make her first basket and at least that long ago when she sold her first one in the Halifax market. Without the market their family tradition of maple-splint baskets would have disappeared long ago.

The oldest face in the market belongs to a man who began selling vegetables nearly eighty years ago at Cheapside. Early every Saturday morning—so early that it was still the night before—he and his grandmother hitched the horse to a wagon loaded with vegetables and set off from Cole Harbour. As they waited to board the ferry, they unhitched the horse and left it behind to save a nickel.

Every Saturday morning Catherine LaPierre and her son Seymour arrived on the same ferry with their wagonload of eggs, butter, beans, peas, beets, wild berries and wild flowers.

The LaPierre family has been selling in Halifax City Market for three generations. Catherine and Rufus LaPierre bought the original Preston homestead in 1895. While he worked full time as a carpenter and she full time as a mother

Right: *Seymour LaPierre, aged eleven, at the Cheapside market, 1903.*
Below: *Catherine LaPierre at Cheapside, about the same date.* Opposite:
*Mary Ann LaPierre in the Halifax market of today.*

raising four children, together they also managed a small,
full-time farm. They tended cows, chickens, pigs and horses,
and cultivated grain for their livestock as well as flowers and
vegetables for the market.

Preparations for the market kept Catherine and her
children busy for most of the week during the summer.
While she churned butter or hoed the large vegetable patch,
they collected eggs and hunted for wild blueberries,
raspberries and blackberries. All day Friday they picked and
trimmed vegetables, filled egg baskets, cut flowers and made
lists of the things the family needed to buy in Halifax. After
supper Seymour loaded the wagon (in winter, the sled) and
at midnight he and his mother joined their neighbours in the
long line of horses and wagons heading for the Dartmouth
ferry, which was seven miles from their Preston farm.

Once they had taken up their regular spot at the
Cheapside market, Catherine would leave her son the
pleasanter task of selling their berries, vegetables and flowers
while she shopped in the nearby stores for sugar, dry goods
and other supplies for the family. When her son was older
and able to deal with the city's shopkeepers, Catherine sent
him off to do the shopping chores while she stayed behind to
sell. She loved the gaiety and bustling activity. It was
possible, though not easy, to talk with a neighbour whose
cart was parked across the street by occasionally shouting
over the endless clamour of hucksters, live poultry and
clanging bells of street trams trying to inch past. In 1916
they were among the reluctant vendors who left the streets
and sidewalks of Cheapside to sell from a stall in the new
market house. Catherine stopped selling regularly in the
Halifax market when she was eighty-five.

Seymour and his wife Joyce took over the family stall
when Catherine retired in 1934. Market gardening was a
major source of income for the second-generation LaPierres.
In the winter Seymour hauled logs from the bush with yoked

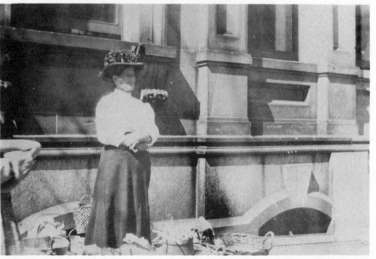

oxen and milled his own lumber. Early in the spring the whole family turned its attention to tending young plants in the hothouse and to planting several acres of vegetables and flowers. Through the summer and late into the fall the weeks were filled with hoeing and picking and preparing for the market. Some things were sold to local grocers and wholesalers, but most of their produce—the hothouse transplants, wild blueberries, strawberries, carrots, parsnips, potatoes and cabbages—were transported to the market house every Friday and Saturday. Patient and talented with a needle, Joyce displayed her fancy work and knitted socks and mittens beside the potatoes and turnips.

The 1940s were good years for all the market people in Halifax. On Fridays when the market stayed open until nine P.M., some customers arriving late had to be turned away. Those were the days, Joyce remembers, when butchers brought whole carcasses of beef into their stalls, where they were skinned and then cut up to order. In the winter when the family had less to sell, Joyce took her needlework and eggs to Halifax on a bus owned by a vendor from Chezzetcook. Joyce LaPierre still sells her fancy needlework in the market, but her daughter Mary Ann is now in charge of the family's stall.

As a young girl on hot summer days Mary Ann shared the berry-picking duties with her sister. Later she took her turn selling in the market. And much later, while working in Halifax, Mary Ann helped with her family's market chores on weekends and in the evenings. Five years ago she decided to become a full-time market gardener.

Mary Ann intensively gardens three acres of the family farm in Preston, growing beans, peas, broad beans, onions, potatoes, Swiss chard, herbs, cucumbers, tomatoes, beets, parsnips, carrots, rhubarb and squash. She buys more of everything from farmers and gardeners close by. All of it is sold in the market in Halifax.

*Basket vendors in Halifax Green Market, c.1905.*

About forty-five hours a week are devoted to her crops and the market. On Thursday mornings in the spring, summer and fall she gathers ripe vegetables from the fields, which her mother then helps to prepare for selling. Early in the afternoon she collects what her neighbours have produced for her; late in the afternoon she trucks a load of vegetables to Halifax. That evening she loads up again and checks that everything is accounted for. The alarm clock is set for 3:30 A.M. On Friday morning by 4:45 Mary Ann is at the market hefting vegetables and setting up tables. From 6:00 to noon she and her mother cheerfully greet and tend to customers. What has not been sold by noon is loaded back on the truck, after the tables are dismantled, and carted back home, where the same routine is repeated at a faster pace for the Saturday morning market.

Though not an easy vocation, producing to sell in the market is a very satisfying one for Mary Ann. Having a market nearby allows her to earn a living doing what she enjoys most: working on the land and meeting her customers face-to-face. She considers the market essential in a city like Halifax. It is the one place where local farmers can keep in touch with the needs and tastes of consumers; where Haligonians can buy the only really fresh fruits and vegetables in the city; and where small farmers can hope to make a decent livelihood.

Because it lacks a permanent location, the market in Halifax is in trouble. Mary Ann and two other vendors have formed a market-sellers' committee to convince city council that the city needs its market, and that if the historic market is to survive it must have a permanent, though modest, market site. The council has agreed to study the future of the market sometime soon.

# 6 Markets in New Brunswick

SAINT JOHN and Fredericton started off on the same foot in the 1780s as Loyalist settlements, but because of geography and circumstances, within a few years they were miles apart in character. Noting the differences that were apparent in the 1790s, one historian has described Saint John as an outward-looking, commercially-oriented city, and Fredericton as an inward-looking community with a bureaucratic and rural perspective. A British visitor to New Brunswick in the mid-nineteenth century praised Saint John, which by then had grown prosperous in the timber trade and was becoming world-famous as a shipbuilding centre, for its enterprise and industry, and criticized Fredericton for exhibiting none of these traits. He saw Saint John as a progressive city and bustling port and its neighbour seventy miles upriver as a small country village with a prevailing attitude of "nonchalance". Even Fredericton's most famous son, Sir Charles G. D. Roberts, reproached his city for being too self-absorbed: "She has sat aloof, Narcissus-like, admiring her own image in her splendid threshold of water, too loftily indifferent to proclaim her merits to the world."

This difference in character is reflected in the cities' markets. There is no other market in Canada quite like the Saint John City Market; its entrepreneurial spirit, which seems to have been there almost from the beginning, has made it unique. Fredericton's Boyce Market is a traditional farmers' market, one of the best community markets in the country—a fact the community has kept to itself.

Within a few months in the spring and summer of 1783 Saint John was transformed from a formidable wilderness into a town one third the size of Boston. The five thousand Loyalist settlers, many of whom had left behind sophisticated city comforts and influential positions as educators, politicians, magistrates and merchants, civilized the wilderness almost as quickly as they tamed it. During their first year a thousand homes were built. In 1784 they had persuaded the Colonial Office in London to separate New Brunswick from Nova Scotia and to create a self-governing colony. In 1785 they convinced George III to give Saint John city status, and their Royal Charter of Incorporation was the first one granted in the British colonies. Other schemes, however, would be thwarted.

The Loyalists had brought with them specific plans for their new settlement. Their ideal was a self-sufficient community with a strong agricultural backbone. Undaunted

when they first faced endless miles of oak and white pine, within a decade they were frustrated by the magnitude of the task at hand. They were lucky if they had managed to clear five acres after ten years of brutalizing drudgery. One prominent Loyalist lamented that "with hardly credit to buy an axe, but a wife, ten children and the gout have held me fast". Another proposed annexation to the United States as a solution to the colony's agricultural backwardness. By 1800 they had changed their original plans and were beginning to hang their hopes for the future on timber and trade rather than on the valley's soil. Saint John thereafter became a community of entrepreneurs rather than of farmers.

Both timber and trade made the city prosperous while discouraging agricultural development in the river valley. It seemed easier and cheaper to import food than to produce it at home. With no steady and enthusiastic demand for their products, farmers had little incentive to improve their skills or alter outmoded habits. They were still engaged in subsistence agriculture years after other colonies had attained a measure of self-sufficiency.

The effect of the timber business was even worse. Farmers were lured away from their land by the irresistible promise of quick cash for wintertime work as teamsters and

lumberjacks. Little time was left for clearing more of their own land, and they often returned to their homesteads late in the spring with bodies so badly beaten by the rigours of the bush that ploughing and planting had to be delayed. That lumbering and farming were not good companions was evident even to a British traveller who visited Saint John in the 1820s: "Wherever the inhabitants are lumberjacks, the country wants all evidences of agricultural development. . . . Who can doubt . . . that the timber business unfits a population, not only for agricultural operations . . . but also generates habits exceedingly prejudicial to their morality and happiness?"

Because Saint John grew up as a community of entrepreneurs (even the farmers were risk-takers, according to a British gentleman who visited the city in the 1820s: "By becoming woodsmen they abandon a certainty to grasp at any imaginary benefit"), its market tradition developed a unique character. From the beginning entrepreneurs and merchants have been prominent figures in the market.

Saint John was granted a common law market privilege in 1785 as part of its Royal Charter of Incorporation. The first market was held in the open air at Market Slip. Sometime in the early decades of the nineteenth century a small frame building was erected at the head of the Slip. A contemporary description of this market mentioned the presence of the lowliest sort of entrepreneur: "There was a weighing machine outside and several hucksters' stands for the sale of cakes, fruit, candy, hard-boiled eggs, gingerbread, apples and pies." In the 1830s the market was being held on the ground floor of a three-story frame building located on the slope of Market Square. Upstairs were the chambers of common council and a public reading room. Downstairs was the very busy shop of a general merchant who sold flour, molasses, tea, tobacco and other necessities imported from Britain, the West Indies and the American states.

The activities and produce of country vendors were seldom mentioned in contemporary accounts of early markets in Saint John, probably because neither was particularly remarkable. Since the farmers were still engaged in subsistence agriculture until at least midway through the nineteenth century, they had very little to spare for the market in the early days. They harvested buckwheat for themselves, Indian corn to sell to lumber camps as workingman's porridge, and potatoes and turnips—most of which was reserved for the family table and to feed a few livestock over the winter. The livestock they could not afford to feed usually ended up in the market. In the winter of 1816 beef and mutton were selling cheap—two cents a pound, hardly worth the long, cold sleigh-ride into the city.

The farmers' trips to market must have been infrequent, due as much to the difficulty of getting there as to the dearth of things to sell. In the first decade of the nineteenth century there was less than twenty miles of navigable road in the entire province. The only means of transporting goods to market was by boat in the summer and by sled in the winter.

Saint John's farmers probably went to market only when it suited them. A regular attendance was certainly less urgent for them than it was for farmers in other communities, such as Charlottetown. For most farmers in early Canada the market was a source of cash, often the only one. But those who worked the soil of the St. John River Valley depended for cash on the timber trade (which was supporting ninety percent of the province by the 1840s). Of course cash was not the only reason farmers in other parts of the country made regular and frequent trips to market; they also recognized a responsibility to provide their community with its basic necessities. This was a responsibility Saint John's farmers had never had to assume. The effect of all this was that the ties of interdependence between city and countryside never developed as strongly in Saint John as in other market communities.

Agriculture stood still until the middle half of the nineteenth century, when it became clear that putting all the community's eggs in one (or two) baskets would eventually threaten its prosperity. Thereafter, farmers, who had been virtually left to fend for themselves for seventy years, received direct encouragement from city merchants and officials and from the colonial government. From the 1850s to the 1870s conditions had changed enough for farmers around Saint John that there was little to distinguish the city's market from markets in other communities of thirty thousand residents. From the tumbledown sheds and stalls clustered along Market Street citizens bought weekly provisions from city butchers and country vendors. With greater quantities and more variety of goods to sell, farmers were less reluctant to make more regular trips to the city. There was a steady demand for their goods in the market and in the shops of the city merchants. And by the 1850s travelling to market was a little less arduous. The roads had been improved somewhat, at least enough to support wagon traffic.

In the 1850s citizens of Saint John began pressing common council to build a new market house. A thousand people had

*The deputy market clerk pulls the market bell which is positioned (right) above his elevated office.*

died from cholera in 1854, and citizens were understandably obsessed with the issue of public health. "The city richly deserved an epidemic," one forthright citizen recalled seventy years later. "We talk of the horrors of the slum sections now, but they are purity itself compared to prominent streets then. Hundreds of domestic animals were kept, it was said, in some cases in the very rooms where the family lived. A dog died on King Street and was left there several days, and dead cats were considered natural features."[1] The hay and livestock markets on King Square added their own natural features to the city streets.

In the midst of all this was the market, where after the epidemic customers became more wary than usual about the odds and ends that might have settled into the sides of pork and kegs of butter they were buying. A new market house, they argued, "would mean a better and more sanitary food supply for the community". The city merchants had their own reasons for supporting the campaign for a new market house. It would attract more farmers into the city and into their shops.

But it could not be just any market house. It had to be a showpiece, the style of building that would tell visitors at a glance that the city was prosperous and enterprising.

Considerable fortunes had been made in timber, ships and the carrying trade, and the market house that was to reflect all this was triumphantly opened in 1876.

It was, boasted a writer for the *Daily Sun*, "a handsome and commodious market house, one of the finest buildings of the kind in Canada". It was certainly commodious, almost four hundred feet from back to front, eighty feet wide and three stories high. Market Street, which ran a full block between Charlotte and Germain streets, became the centre aisle of the new building. Down this middle aisle were enough benches to accommodate a hundred farmers. Permanent shops and stalls for butchers and merchants lined the sides of the great hall.

Its style was even grander than its proportions. The brick facade was adorned with stone facings and pillars and topped off with a high mansard roof. Inside light streamed down through a full-length expanse of arched windows. The hand-hewn timbers and arched oak beams overhead were fashioned by shipbuilders to resemble the inverted hull of a ship.

Once the citizens of Saint John had shopped in their new market house, they quickly forgot its price tag. "It meant an expenditure of $150,000, but it was a thing that could not be

*The impressive timber-arched construction of the market's roof is echoed in
the semi-circular windows below.*

done without. . . . It can be claimed for the market building that it is one of the most useful and ornamental buildings in town." Within a few years, however, its price tag and its usefulness would become the cause of considerable anxiety. A decade after the market house was built, many farmers from the countryside around Saint John would stop making regular trips to the market.

New railway and steamship lines opened up larger markets for valley farmers. The Belleisle farmers were among the first to disappear from the city market. They loaded their produce on board the steamer and sent it to the wholesalers' market at Indiantown, "where it was snapped up by commission men and retail grocers of the city and Portland". A reporter describing the market at Christmastime in 1883 mentioned that noticeably fewer farmers were bothering to come to the market. "The market was better supplied than at any other time since last Christmas," he wrote. "The countrymen from all parts of Kings, Queens and St. Johns counties brought supplies in. In former years produce from the North Shore and Carleton counties were brought in in very large quantities, but of late years all this produce has been sent either to Moncton, Halifax or the U.S."

The market was simply no longer the best way for farmers to sell their produce, and they continued to withdraw from the market. Since their ties to the community's market had never been especially strong, they left with an easy conscience. A century after the splendid new market house was built, there was only one farmer selling there regularly, and he had entrepreneurial interests outside the market which made daily selling feasible. A dozen or so country vendors now rent space in the centre aisle when it is convenient and profitable, when crowds of customers gather on summer weekends and on holidays.

As farmers began disappearing from the market in the last few decades of the nineteenth century, shopkeepers who rented permanent stalls started to sell more of their old standbys. Customers were just as likely to visit the shop of George W. Slocum, Commission Merchant, for their weekly supply of butter and eggs as wait for a farmer to show up in the middle aisle. Mr. Slocum opened his shop in the city market in 1885 and sold wholesale goods on consignment, mostly butter and venison. An agreeable man by nature and scrupulously fair and reliable in his dealings with customers, he was successful in his small shop selling the same things the farmers had sold. By 1900 business was promising enough to take on John Ferris as a partner and to expand their stock to include eggs, cheese and a whole range of country produce. His son Ottie Slocum kept meticulous records of the firm's transactions in a small loft above the shop. Among the expenses for a typical week in 1918 ($12 for rent and $27 for wages) Ottie carefully noted the quarter it had cost him for carfare. Other purchases made that week included five pounds of sausage for $1.15, thirty-one pounds of rhubarb for 35¢ and five 300-pound barrels of turnips for $1.00 each.

The "Fancy Groceries" shop of Slocum & Ferris is still open for business every market day. Although the shop has changed hands (employees of the original family of owners now operate it), little else has changed in almost a century. Customers are still greeted by the same welcoming sign above the shop door: "Through this door pass the finest people, Our Customers, Our Friends".

Though few shops have been operating as long as this one, a number of others have been there for twenty or thirty years, certainly longer than any family of country vendors. What is striking about this market is its lack of third- and fourth-generation vendors. Butchers, fishmongers, shopkeepers and small-time retailers have given this market the sense of continuity that in other markets, particularly ones such as Halifax and Charlottetown, has come from generations of farming families and market gardeners.

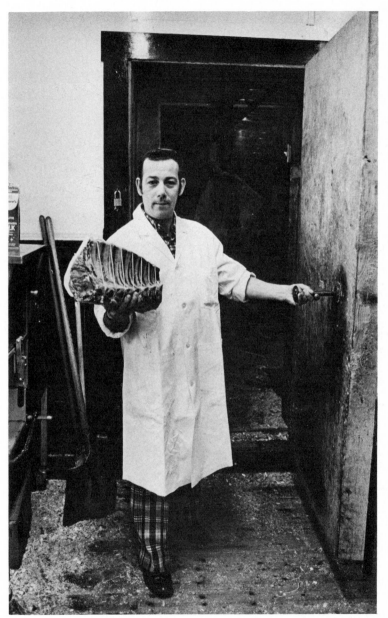

Without them the Saint John City Market might well have disappeared years ago.

Early in the 1970s, when the market was losing almost ten thousand dollars a year, a community planning committee suggested that the market house be demolished and the market moved to more appropriate (smaller) quarters. A citizens' campaign to save the historic and handsome market house won an overwhelming victory. The campaign made the people of Saint John look at their market carefully for the first time in years, and many of them were disappointed. They remembered days when the centre aisle had been crowded with fine, fat geese, bunches of wild mayflowers, and mounds of cabbages and cucumbers. Now when they looked down the aisle what they saw for most of the year were plaster-of-paris Beethovens, ceramic geese and plastic flowers. They complained about the market's commercialism, lamented the "loss of its traditional character", and wondered where all the farmers had gone.

When attacked the market people are quick to defend themselves and their market. "This is a daily market. You're not going to find farmers around here with time to come in every day. They're big-time potato farmers mostly, and they make a good living at that. They're sure not going to get ahead coming in here to sell potatoes every day. Others who want to come, they come when it suits them. Those who don't, don't. The market has been like this for a long, long time. I sure can't remember when it was much different than it is now. And if you talk to the right people in the city, our customers who come to the market regularly, they'll tell you they love it here. Sure, you get some bellyachers complaining about all the knickknacks and so on, but I'll bet you a bag of dulse that they don't know this market, that they don't come more than once a year. There aren't enough farmers willing to sell here every day to keep this market going. Without the knickknacks there wouldn't be a market. They support the farmers' end of the market. Commercialism, hell. This is free enterprise."

While the "bellyachers" see the Saint John City Market as less than a true farmers' market, the market people and most visitors see it as more than just a farmers' market. On the weekends, when the country vendors come in with their fruits and vegetables, it is primarily a farmers' market. During the week, when the knickknacks, plastic flowers and wicker baskets crowd the centre aisle, it is a lively and gregarious bazaar, much like those of the Old World with their hucksters loudly competing for the customers' attention.

In the early 1840s a Presbyterian clergyman from Scotland made an extensive tour of New Brunswick "to point out places where the man of property may invest his capital in the purchase of lands, the mechanic and labourer find employment, and the emigrant a settlement". While he had nothing but praise for the opportunities that Saint John offered, his impressions of Fredericton were less than enthusiastic. After enumerating Fredericton's highpoints—a small but respectable university; Province Hall, a solid but "unpretending edifice"; a Presbyterian parish of admirable size; three banks; an alms-house; and excellent barracks—he candidly set forth the town's shortcomings. It was certainly a civilized town, but it lacked industry and enterprise:

It is only to be decried, that the time is not far distant, when her inhabitants will avail themselves of those facilities afforded by the proximity of water-power, to establish manufactories and machinery. . . . Thus, eligibly situated, it is certainly to be regretted that it is not more distinguished for enterprise, and that it is destitute of these useful institutions which exercise so beneficial an effect upon society, and without which, its members must be deficient of that intelligence and liberality that characterize the present age.

. . . It is also a misfortune for the place that efforts are not made to arrest a large portion of the trade of the upper part of the Province on its way to St John. . . . Persons of stated incomes, and others who can afford it, procure the principal part of their supplies and clothing from Halifax, [Saint John], and even from England and the United States; although there is an abundance of cultivated and excellent land in the vicinity of the town, and settlements are rising up continually at no great distance above and around it.[2]

This gentleman strongly objected to the manner in which the people of Fredericton conducted their business. "Labouring men and mechanics", he complained, were not paid in cash wages but "chiefly out of shop", a system that "acts unjustly on those who are not disposed, or are not situated as to pay in this way". Fredericton's backwardness, he argued, was directly attributable to this reliance on credit rather than cash.

When individuals are hired, they should be paid for their labour in cash, and allowed to purchase any articles they may require, when that can be done to best advantage. If those who reside in the neighbourhood of the place have any debts to pay, or agricultural produce to dispose of, instead of as at present, taking it to a shop where they are indebted, or where an apparently high price is given, payment being made in goods at an advanced rate to meet it; this should be carried to a public market, and there sold upon the best terms, and the party should pay his debts in money, and make his purchase in a similar way. Were this healthy state of business to prevail, much of the present cause of complaint would vanish—competition would be introduced, and the exorbitant rate of living must be materially reduced.

From its situation, Fredericton ought to be a place of excellent business, and should be abundantly supplied with provisions; but at present the former is confined to retail trade, and advances to lumbering parties, while the place is irregularly supplied with fresh provisions; and although there

*Only the occasional load of hay and perhaps a few cattle were sold in Fredericton's earliest market, c.1790.*

is a large market-house in Fredericton, yet there is but one butcher in it, and only three bakers in the town.

Though this Scottish gentleman proposed that because of its method of conducting business "Fredericton exhibits a state of society not to be equalled in North America", it seems likely that the town was neither unique nor especially backward. Most other townspeople in the early years of settlement relied on shopkeepers' credit, and not many communities with only four thousand residents had more than one butcher selling in the market house.

There is certainly nothing special about the history of the market to suggest that Fredericton suffered any more economic crises than other small, isolated communities. Until recently there was nothing particularly remarkable about Fredericton's market. The first market was set up soon after Fredericton was named provincial capital in 1785. The timber trade slowed down agricultural development until the mid-nineteenth century, but by the 1840s, seventeen hundred acres in the surrounding countryside were being cultivated, and farmers were travelling to town every few weeks in the summer and fall to sell their produce and hay in the town's public square. When Fredericton became a city in 1848, one of the first motions put before the new council was "to enquire and report upon the best means of providing a market in some part of the city above Carleton Street, and also to enquire and report upon the necessary market regulations for Fredericton". After two years and too many other financial obligations, council's only progress was its decision to erect a market house on Phoenix Square. In 1850 Fredericton's market house was built, but the city had overextended itself. A year later the council ordered that "a new Market Committee together with His Worship the Mayor be a Committee to enquire, ascertain and finally determine what arrangements can be made by the city for paying the amount due to the contractor". The mayor

negotiated a £250 loan, which was to be repaid from "rents of the Ordinance Lands and Hospital Lots" and by renting the top floor of the market house to the Young Men's Total Abstinence Society.

In the 1860s Fredericton was operating separate produce and livestock, hay, fish, and cordwood markets. These markets must have been doing a considerable business: competition was stiff for jobs as toll collectors and market inspectors. In 1863 when the tenders were all in, Mr. P. McDevitt was appointed toll collector of the haymarket "at a rate of five percent commission", and Mr. Thomas Hicks won the job of inspector of the cordwood market. A few years later Mr. Bernard McCafferty was the highest bidder (at $100) for the office of Clerk of Phoenix Square Market and Weigh Scales. The butchers' stalls in the Phoenix Square Market were auctioned off every year, and competition for space sometimes resulted in a free-for-all.

In the late 1860s it was as clear in Fredericton as in Saint John that the new railway and steamship lines and the wholesale trade were affecting market business. In 1866 Mr. R. Forsyth, Collector of the King's Ward Market tolls, petitioned city council "to have his liabilities reduced due to

MARKETS IN NEW BRUNSWICK  67

changes in market patterns and the shipment of most meat to the U.S.".

These changes in the way produce and livestock were distributed reduced the size of Fredericton's market, as they did in Saint John. From the late nineteenth century to 1951, the market was small and orderly enough to operate in the basement of City Hall. In 1951 W. W. Boyce, a prominent businessman in the community, donated funds to erect a plain and functional market house in an old neighbourhood of elm-lined streets and fanciful frame houses.

Fredericton's market never lost as many country vendors as did the Saint John City Market. In 1972 when only a dozen farmers rented weekend space in the Saint John market, almost thirty vendors were selling produce in the Boyce Market. And unlike Saint John's vendors, many in Fredericton were second- and third-generation. One homemade-jam-and-jelly vendor has been selling in Fredericton's market for fifty years. She started as a child picking wild strawberries on land that had been recently cleared and burned, and heaping them in wooden pails she carried from a yoke.

According to the Boyce's Market Clerk, 1972 was a turning point for the market. That year he began running the affairs of the market. Eight years later 120 stalls are rented out to eighty vendors. With a very clear idea of what a contemporary public market ought to be, he devoted most of his time to attracting new vendors and bringing better quality and more variety into the market. There is no doubt that he has been successful.

Fredericton's Boyce Market is everything a traditional farmers' market should be. It is financially successful, with fifty thousand dollars changing hands most market days. It is filled with an impressive variety of locally-grown produce and cottage-industry crafts, from Harold Love's whole pigs, the Walton family's fresh lamb, Mactaquac Farms' "old-fashioned home-smoked hams and bacons", natural yogurt, apple cider, maple candy and firewood to handmade sisal baskets, leatherwork, handspun wool and knitted socks. Its vendors are professional and energetic with a strong commitment to the market tradition. When the market opens its doors every Saturday morning, an eager, gregarious crowd of customers is lined up outside. All of Fredericton seems to turn up every market day, from the family across the street to the provincial premier. The market is as much a community centre and a weekly social event as a place to buy lettuce and onions.

Though considerably smaller, Fredericton's Boyce Market certainly measures up to Kitchener Farmers' Market, which is reputed to be the best farmers' market in Canada. But there is one striking difference. The Kitchener market is a world-famous tourist attraction, a featured highlight on all guided tours of the city. Fredericton, on the other hand, has kept its market a well-guarded secret, perhaps to preserve its special character as a gathering place for the community.

# 7 Markets in Quebec

**M**ONTREAL and Quebec were major stopping places for travellers in the nineteenth century, especially for British and American tourists who came to bask in the colourful French-Canadian culture. "Colourful" and "picturesque" were two of their favourite adjectives, and so were "backward" and "primitive". George Munro Grant, describing French-Canadian life and character for an American audience in 1899, was a typical visitor and his perspective typically Anglo-American: "The French Canadians cling to the most primitive methods in this [maple sugaring in particular, and farming in general], as in everything else, the result, if an economic loss, being at least a picturesque gain."[1]

Nothing in these cities was more colourful and picturesque than their markets. The Quebec City Market received extensive coverage in Jeremy Cockloft's *Cursory Observations made in Quebec, Province of Lower Canada in the Year 1811:*

> At the dawn of day, which at this season of the year, being the month of July, breaks very early, I was awakened by a confused noise in the street below; which, upon quitting my hole and applying to the window in the open part of the garret, which looked into the street, I found the whole of it crowded with a number of carts and vociferous Charioteers, as they are termed.° A Frenchman is naturally noisy; but the Canadian Charioteers! Heaven defend me from *them*! I have heard the jackalls in the woods of Hindostan,—I have witnessed the chattering herds of monkeys on the coast of Malay,—but their howlings and chatterings were *music* to the sounds which now assailed my ears.—To endeavor to sleep was useless; I therefore huddled on my clothes, hurried down stairs, and made the best of my way to what is called the Lower-town Market. It is fortunate for the people of Quebec, that the coolness of their climate preserves them from those infectious disorders which emanate from the dirt and filth of both animal and vegetable putrefaction. As it was early, I found the four or five butchers' stalls, being the only ones in the market, in the same situation as they were left on the preceding Saturday. The Market-house under which they are placed, is an old wooden building, with a shingled roof; round this are affixed posts, with rings to accommodate the 'Habitants in making fast their calves, pigs, sheep, oxen, &c. which they bring to market to vend to the butchers;—the remainder of the market-place is an oblong square, about 200 feet in length and 120 in breadth, the market-house standing about one third from the SW part of the square, and

° Charioteer is a term among the Canadians for truckmen, and Calesch and Cariole drivers.

*Scenes from the Champlain market, c.1911.*

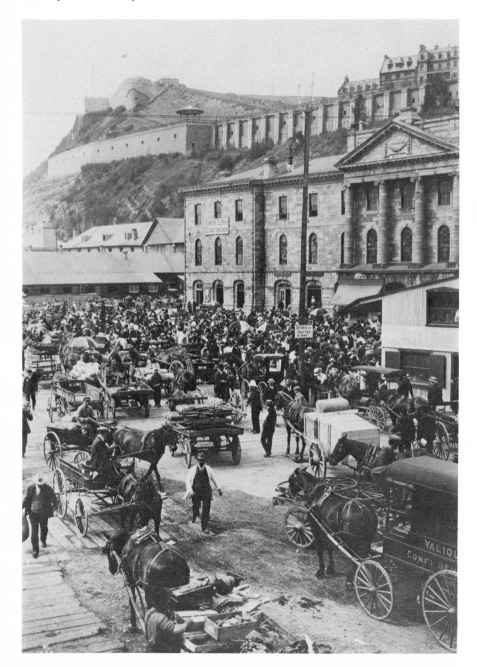

extending about two thirds of the length. This whole area was covered with the refuse of vegetables;—in a warm climate, they would certainly have been productive of disease to the surrounding inhabitants; and the stench of them here must create disagreeable feelings. I had scarcely finished these observations, when I saw some 'Habitants in red night-caps, dragging a few lean calves and sheep to the rings before mentioned;—As they have sense enough to know that these animals naturally move head foremost, they fasten a line round their necks, and drag them, *nolens, volens*, from the river to the market. I have seen some of these poor animals almost strangled by this *humane* method;—but the 'Habitant smokes his pipe with all the *sang froid* imaginable, and with hauling and repeated *marche donc*,° drags the animal to the post;—not so with Mr. Hog,—he will not put up with such treatment; and therefore is generally bound all four feet together. Now gentle reader, figure in imagination, oxen lowing, calves bleating, sheep bal-ing, [sic] hogs squeaking, squealing and grunting, ducks quacking, fowls cackling; and last of all, and by far the most noisy, Canadians jabbering;— and all this an hour before sun-rise of a summer's morning,— and you will have some slight conception what a charming serenade this must be, and how gratifying and pleasing to the inhabitants of the houses round the market-place; especially should any of them be sick. The general purchasers in this market are those concerned with the shipping, boarding-house keepers, and residents in the Lower Town, who do not seem to dislike or take much notice of the slovenly and dirty condition in which the different articles are generally offered for sale. The sun was just rising, when I was accosted by a tall, thin figure, of a most livid aspect, whom I found to be Mr. R. my landlord. He called my attention to every thing which he thought superb; and in the true spirit of a Frenchman, asked me if I had seen any thing like such a market before? I answered him, and that truly, that I had never seen any thing like it, even in London. He made me a

bow; it was a bow of gratitude;—he felt pleased,—and I made him so. I enquired the road to Break-neck-stairs, as from thence I could easily find my way to the Upper Town, or more properly the Hidalgo Market. This market is so named, because it is generally frequented by officers in the army, and in different civil departments under government. The butchers even, seem to emulate their customers in politeness, as far as their savage natures will admit; as you will observe here and there a clean white apron amongs them:—their meat better dressed and cut in a much neater manner than in the lower town. The building is circular, and the roof forms a cupola, commencing from the ground;—the butchers' stalls are fixed round the walls on the inside; and in the centre fruit and vegetables are sold by those who have permission, which is obtained by purchase. There is a foot-path around it, and on the outside of this, the carts of the 'Habitants are ranged, to the number generally of about a hundred;—but do not let my readers suppose that these vehicles are loaded with the productions of the garden or even the field;—to cut the matter short, they are not loaded at all. The 'Habitant may have two or three bunches of onions, as many of turnips and carrots; half a dozen baskets of wild strawberries, raspberries and currants; which, with a dozen eggs and a bushel of potatoes, compose in general the whole of his freight, and which he has brought four or five miles to dispose of. Thus the man, with his horse and cart, is employed the whole day in vending three or four dollars worth of vegetables;— However, it agrees with their natural indolence; and whilst the 'Habitant can quietly smoke his pipe, he cares little about the sale of his merchandize. The market closes about mid-day. The French language is most essential in marketing, as an English tongue is sure to enhance the price with the 'Habitant, he being perfectly acquainted with the liberal disposition of Englishmen, and knows that the price is seldom an obstacle to John Bull when the gratification of his appetite is in question.[2]

° *Marche donc* is a term used by Canadian drivers, answering to our English term "Get on!"

Left: *Upper-Town Marketplace, Quebec City, 1870s.*
*Bonsecours, Montreal, 1922.*

William Kirby, author of *The Golden Dog* (a novel about Quebec in the days of Bigot) was born in England, emigrated to the United States in 1832 and seven years later to Canada. In 1839, on a visit to Quebec City, he too described the vibrant life in the market, but without the long-nosed condescension of Mr. Cockloft:

> We visited the old market opposite the French Cathedral and admired the busy scene. The habitant men and women, the former dressed in etoffe du pays, with blue and red toques on their heads, and colored sashes around their waists. The women in gay calicoes and wide straw hats, handsome, rosy and loquacious, presiding over the sale of butter and eggs, fruits and vegetables. The boys of the Seminary dressed in blue coats edged with white cord, and wearing green sashes; soldiers in red coats mingled with priests in broad hats, black soutanes or gowns; nuns with their strange headgear, and the good wives of Quebec, busy doing their marketing. It was a gay and animated scene, until modern civic Vandals tore down the venerable Jesuit College and removed the market to another place.[3]

The markets in Montreal also had their full share of Anglo-American visitors in the nineteenth century. The city's original marketplace was laid out in 1676, and continued to be the centre of the community's commercial and social life until the first decade of the nineteenth century. Had there been as many visitors in the seventeenth century as later, they too would probably have raved about the market's picturesqueness. But for descriptions of Montreal's early market we must be satisfied with the imaginative recreations of nineteenth-century writers: "The savages that frequent the great lakes came down with prodigious quantities of beaver skins, which they gave in exchange for arms, kettles, axes, etc., upon which the merchants generally cleared 200 percent."[4]

The market was moved to Jacques Cartier Square in 1803. Though there were plans to build a market house in 1807, insufficient funds forced a compromise. Forty temporary stalls were erected to keep the wind and rain off the butchers. A frame building appeared several years later, to which a new wing was added in 1821. The Bonsecours Market House was built in 1842 to replace this inadequate and somewhat shabby structure. No visitor to Montreal failed

to be impressed by the new building's imposing style and dimensions. In 1870 Alfred Sandham added his praise to the others. The Bonsecours Market House, he wrote, "was a magnificent pile of cut stone buildings in the Grecian-Doric style of architecture, erected at a cost of $200,000, and equal, if not superior, to any building of the kind in America." Mr. Sandham was not a typical visitor. He lived in Quebec and knew Montreal well. While he too appreciated the colourfulness of its markets, he was more astounded by the size of their profits.

When Mr. Sandham wrote about Montreal in the late 1860s, the city was operating eight public markets. Bonsecours was the largest and most profitable. In 1868, when the population of Montreal had reached 100,000, he reported that $195,000 worth of farm produce was being sold annually in the Bonsecours Market. Tallying revenues and expenditures for 1868, he noted that the city was pocketing more than $20,000 in profit, which was a 10 percent return on their investment.

St. Ann's Market was doing almost as well, showing a profit of slightly less than 10 percent. The market house was built in 1851 for $82,000 and accommodated 56 butchers as

well as a large and fluctuating number of country vendors. In 1868, $150,000 changed hands in the brick, two-story market house.

The St. Lawrence Market was erected on Main Street in 1861 at a cost of $24,000. Twenty thousand dollars worth of staples, mostly vegetables and poultry, was sold from 45 stalls in 1868, leaving the city with a 15 percent profit. Although this was a relatively new market, Mr. Sandham indicated that it was "liberally patronized by the people of this improving neighbourhood".

The St. Antoine Market on Mountain Street was also built in 1861. Annual revenues from renting 40 butchers' stalls, from leasing space to country vendors and from tolls collected for use of the public scales was $4,000, and expenditures amounted to $1,500. This was the least profitable market with profits hovering at 6 percent.

The St. Gabriel Market at Point St. Charles (also built in 1861) was primarily a cattle market. The population of the area was small, and only $2,000 worth of produce and meat was sold annually in its early years. Though its profit margin was slim, the city still considered it a good investment.

The Papineau Market led the others with an 18 percent

profit, but most of its revenues came from the weighing of hay and straw. There was also a cattle market on Craig Street, which included a brick market house and "commodious sheds for the reception and sale of livestock", and a haymarket which occupied a plot of land that had originally been a walled garden.

Mr. Sandham was impressed when he tallied the annual surplus revenues from "the *bona fide* butchers' markets" (Bonsecours, St. Ann's, St. Lawrence and St. Antoine). The city pocketed almost $35,000 in 1868, an average profit of 10 percent. More than half a million dollars worth of farm produce was sold in six markets, and the fish market added another $193,000 to the total sales.

In the 1870s few markets in Canada could begin to compare with Montreal's in terms of volume of business. Fewer still came close to matching their 10 percent profit figure. George Munro Grant, who so confidently wrote in 1899 that at least the French-Canadians' economic losses were balanced by their picturesque gains, saw in French-Canadian character only what he was predisposed to see.

# 8 Ottawa's Byward Market

"THERE'S no doubt in my mind that Byward is one of the best markets in Canada. I've been to markets in Kitchener, London, Kingston and Toronto. This one isn't as big as some of those, but aside from that, it measures up pretty well. It sure can't be beat in the spring and summer when all the flowers are out on display. Tulips and glads and mums, and just about anything else you can think of. Banks of them everywhere. It's really a beautiful sight to behold.

"This is a very old market. Must be one of the oldest. It started up in 1829, and I'm pretty sure it's been operating non-stop since then. It's moved around a bit. We've got a write-up on this market that says that Colonel By built a market house on Lyon Street in 1829. It sure was cheap to build in those days. The market house cost less than a thousand dollars, if I remember right. Another one opened a while later on George Street in Lower Town. That wouldn't be too far from here. This building was built sometime in the 1870s. It burned about fifty years later, but it was soon fixed up. Probably completely rebuilt. I started coming to the market in this building right here. About forty, maybe closer to fifty, years ago. As a young lad with my mother.

"I used to be a vendor until a few years ago. Now I'm retired and taking it easy. Don't do too much of anything, I guess. Except come down here a lot. Some of my old friends are still selling here, and I come down to pass the time of day with them. And to buy from them, of course. You can't beat the fine stuff they're selling here in the market. You know it's fresh and where it's coming from. Beats me why the whole city doesn't come down here to buy their groceries. At least their produce. I have to laugh when I see people buying peas and sweet corn in a supermarket. They start to lose their flavour and sweetness as soon as they're picked. It's best to have your pot boiling even before you pick them. The closest you're going to get to that is to buy them here, when they've been picked the morning they're being sold.

"Yes, I started coming here with Mother. That's way before you were born. It was during the Depression. My family, and just about everybody else's, was damned poor in those days. If my folks had a couple of nickels to rub together, they thought they were lucky. We didn't starve, but we sure didn't see much cash. That's one of the reasons we went to the market. Cash.

"My dad was a farmer. And a pretty good one. He worked a hundred acres and raised pigs and sheep and cows for

Top: *Wood market in Ottawa, 1918; fruit market, 1922.* Bottom: *Ottawa market, 1921.*

milking. He was really a horse man, though. Horses were his first love. He had quite a reputation in the county for his horse-training talents. That's what got us through the Depression. That and Mother's hens and garden.

"Every spring Dad went out and got two young Percherons. I don't know how he got them, whether he traded them for something else or bought them outright. Can't recall how he managed that. They weren't broken yet. That was his job. He worked with that pair, breaking them in, getting them used to the harness and working together, until the following spring. Then he sold them, sometimes back to the fellow he'd got them from in the first place, or to somebody else who needed a team for ploughing. That's the way he got the money to pay for the mortgage and the taxes. There were lots of our neighbours who weren't so lucky as my folks. A lot of farms were repossessed in those days.

"Mother kept chickens, geese and ducks, and tended a huge garden. That woman was the best gardener I've ever seen. Her cabbages weighed fifteen pounds apiece. Her gooseberries were the size of banty eggs. Well almost, anyway. I remember asking Mother about the birds and the bees when I was really young. She told me she'd found all her babies in the gooseberry patch. I went out and looked through that patch every day that summer. I didn't find what I was looking for, but I sure ate a lot of gooseberries.

"My older brothers helped Dad with the farm chores. The younger kids helped Mother in the garden—planting, hoeing, weeding and picking. We were out there every day as soon as the dew was off. After that we gathered the eggs. The day before we went to market was hectic. Mother wanted everything to look nice, so we dusted off all the vegetables and cleaned all the eggs. We worked hard from early morning to late at night. After supper the whole family sat around the table. Mother and Dad made a list of things they needed to buy in the city, and all the kids were busy dusting and cleaning and packing up.

"Sometimes we didn't have too much other than the eggs. But in the spring and summer there were the vegetables and berries. In the late fall, after Dad had butchered a few pigs, we were loaded. Those nights neither Dad nor Mother went to bed at all. There were pumpkins, squash, beets, cabbages, eggs, sausages, sides of pork, and hens, geese and ducks to pack up and worry about.

They woke the kids at three in the morning. We sat around the table eating porridge and sipping steamy cups of tea. Then the young ones were bundled up in quilts and loaded onto the wagon with everything else. Then we were off to the market.

"Mother always wanted to be in the market bright and early so she'd have plenty of time to set up. She spent a lot of time arranging her vegetables so they'd look nice and tempting. Even though it was the Depression, and people didn't have much money to spend. Those were lean years, all right, but people could still appreciate a fine-looking apple or bunch of carrots. Her customers always appreciated the time she spent on her display, and she had more customers than any other vendor.

"Our regular customers showed up every week as soon as the market was open. And they usually had the same order. Potatoes, cabbages and eggs, mostly. A lot of turnips and maybe some berries when they were in season. Most people pretty well lived from week to week. They couldn't afford to buy in big quantities, like most folks do now. No, they filled their baskets or carpetbags with as much bulk as they could afford for the money they had. Amazing to think now that a whole family could get along on a basketful of groceries from one market day to the next.

"Of course, some of Mother's regular customers couldn't

84 TO MARKET, TO MARKET

afford to pay right away. So she'd let them go and mark their purchases in a scribbler. What else could she do but give a family credit and trust them to repay when they could? Especially when there were six skinny kids hanging onto their mother's skirts and looking at the berries or eggs with big, hungry eyes. She didn't turn them away, and I don't think she could have even if she'd wanted to.

"One family, I remember, ran up quite a bill one summer. She didn't have the heart to cut them off. In the fall they still didn't have the money to pay her, so the man came out to the farm and helped my dad repair our barn and sheds.

"There was quite a bit of stealing in the market when times were really bad. Some folks had no other way of getting food for the table. I remember one day Mother caught this little urchin stuffing eggs into his jacket when she turned to deal with another customer. She let him have about three or four before she sent him on his way. But there were some thieves she couldn't abide. The really greedy ones, I guess. She let one fellow get away with something small once. But then he kept coming back. One morning she rapped him across the head with the handle of her whip and swore she'd give him the other end if he ever showed up again. He didn't.

"Maybe I'm sentimental, but those were the good old days in the market. It was sure great for kids. After we helped Mother set up her table, we went off to join the other kids. We were a funny-looking gang—pants too short, patched over three times in one spot, shoes handed down and three sizes too big. One of my pals didn't even have shoes to wear in the winter. A couple of sacks tied at the ankles was all he had one year. And he wasn't the only one. Sometimes we even made a little money, a penny, and if we were really lucky, maybe two. We used to search through the market for rich ladies and offered to carry their groceries home. They weren't hard to spot. In fact, they stood out like sore thumbs.

All dressed up in big, heavy hats and gingerly stepping around the mess the horses left behind. There weren't too many of those ladies, though. You had to be good to spot them first.

"There's been a lot of changes here since then. There were years when the market wasn't too popular. Mostly in the fifties and sixties when we couldn't compete with supermarkets. They were so neat and clean. And that's when all the vendors here were selling only their own produce. When our tomatoes and cucumbers still had a month left on the vine, the supermarkets and grocery stores were hauling truckloads of ripe ones from Niagara and even Leamington. That's changed. Vendors can buy produce from those areas to resell in the market. And the vendors now have an organization to promote the market.

"The biggest change, of course, you can see right in front of you. The vendors don't sell inside the market house anymore. The building was fixed up a few years back, and they couldn't afford to pay the kinds of rents the city needed to keep it up. So it was turned into a place for craftsmen and artists. Sort of a gallery, I guess you'd call it. Some people complained, of course. But I don't think any of them offered any hard-and-fast solutions. The way it is now, it attracts more people into this area. Before, people thought this was a pretty sleazy area. So that's a good change. You can't have a market unless you've got customers.

"Considering what it was like twenty years ago, I think the market's improved. But it'll never be as good as it was when I was a young lad."

# 9 Toronto's St. Lawrence Market

ON November 5, 1803, the Lieutenant Governor of Upper Canada announced in the *Gazette* the opening of a public market in the Town of York:

Whereas great prejudice hath arisen to the Inhabitants of the Town and Township of York, and of other adjoining Townships, from no place or day having been set apart or appointed for exposing publicly for Sale, Cattle, Sheep, Poultry, and other Provisions, Goods and Merchandize, brought by Merchants, Farmers, and others, for the necessary supply of the said Town of York;

And Whereas great benefit and advantage might be derived to the said Inhabitants and others, by establishing a Weekly Market within that Town, at a place and on a day certain for the purpose aforesaid—KNOW ALL MEN, That I, PETER HUNTER, Esquire, Lieutenant Governor of the said Province, taking the Premises into consideration, and willing to promote the interest, advantage and accommodation of the Inhabitants of the Town and Township aforesaid, and of others His Majesty's Subjects within the said Province, by and with the advice of the Executive Council thereof, have ordained, erected, established and appointed, and do hereby ordain, erect, establish and appoint, A PUBLIC OPEN MARKET, to be held on SATURDAY, in each and every week during the year, within the said Town of York: (The first market to be held therein on SATURDAY, the FIFTH DAY OF NOVEMBER next, after the date of these Presents) on a certain piece or plot of Land within the Town, consisting of five Acres and a half, commencing at the South-east angle of the said plot, at the corner of Market [Wellington] Street and New [Jarvis] Street, then North sixteen degrees West five chains seventeen links, more or less, to King's Street; then along King Street South seventy-four degrees West nine chains fifty one links, more or less, to Market [Church] Street; then along Market Street North seventy-four degrees East two chains; then North sixty-four degrees East along Market Street seven chains sixty links, more or less, to the place of beginning—for the purpose of exposing for Sale, CATTLE, SHEEP, POULTRY, and other Provisions, GOODS and MERCHANDIZE, as aforesaid.

The original St. Lawrence Market was a long, low wooden building constructed in the centre of the square to house the town's butchers. Half carcasses of beef and whole stiff pigs, a little on the lean side, swung from iron hooks down the full thirty-six-foot length of the shambles. Outside in the open square were crude pens to hold the farmers' livestock— worn-out ewes, fat bullocks and skinny swine that had been browsing in the bush all winter. Horses and oxen were tethered to hitching posts that ran around the perimeter of

*View of Toronto, 1894, looking northwest from Front and Sherbourne streets, showing the haymarket and weigh scales, far left.*

the square. Everywhere were squawking hens; six or so were bound together by the feet and left to tumble about on the ground.

Almost everyone in town turned out for market day. The busiest days were those on which some poor wretch was being sent to the pillory or the stocks or the whipping post set up in the square. In April 1804 Elizabeth Ellis was hanging her head in the pillory, convicted of "keeping a disorderly house" (her husband was acquitted). She had been sentenced to six months in jail and "to stand in the pillory twice during the said imprisonment, on two different maket days, opposite the Market House in the Town of York, for the space of two hours at a time". Ely Playter, on his way to town that morning, noted the crowds of market people rushing to the square in time to see the woman put into the pillory. "Though the day was pleasant," he said, "Mr. Fisk, who was chosen High Constable, made a very rediculous [*sic*] appearance at the impilloring [of] the poor woman."

Every Saturday the shops along King and Market streets closed down between six A.M. and four P.M. While the market was open no one was allowed to sell provisions of any kind except in market square. At the market's closing bell shopkeepers reopened their stores, and families lined up inside and outside for souchong tea, kegs of vinegar and loaves of sugar. Children dug deep into the penny candy jars; young girls fingered the satin and china ribbons; young boys gawked at the soft leather boots and the morocco slippers.

The market was a success from the beginning and soon became known as the "best-supplied and most commodious market in Upper Canada". What made it thrive, especially at the outset, was the fact that farmers could get cash for their produce. In most other towns in Upper Canada goods were still bartered in the local markets because money was scarce. York was a government town. The government purchased supplies for the garrison with cash; military

*St. Lawrence Hall, 1855.*

*St. Lawrence Market, 1919.*

officers and civil servants had cash to buy their weekly groceries. Farmers came from settlements around Markham and Newmarket with their wagons loaded down with vegetables and fruit and chickens. The prospect of a journey down mud-holed, stump-infested Yonge Street kept none of them away when the jingle of a pocketful of cash sounded in their heads.

On market days Yonge Street traffic was heavy. Resigned to the inevitability of being mired to the axles in mud, farmers good-naturedly joined their neighbours in the wagon train which gingerly manoeuvred its way to town. When one of the wagons got stuck deep in a mud-wallow, the others in the caravan helped unload it, hitch the team of oxen to its stern, drag it out backwards and look for the best way around the troublesome spot.

Having a good market close by encouraged the Yonge Street farmers to diversify. In other areas of the province where no local markets were set up, where roads were even worse than Yonge Street, farmers concentrated on growing grain, mostly wheat, which they sold to merchants and shopkeepers. Farmers who could manage regular trips to York were soon doubling their poultry yards and expanding their kitchen gardens to produce potatoes, cabbages, peas an beans for the townspeople who assembled every Saturday in the market. Though they were not especially concerned about the breed of their livestock—those that could stand starvation best were considered optimal—the farmers did consider sheltering them in the winter so they would be more than skin and bones when they arrived at the market.

The cash these farmers received from the market was not long in their pockets. Almost all of it went to pay for the necessities they had been buying all year from York's shopkeepers. Most farmers were heavily indebted to the general merchants in town, especially to prosperous ones such as William Allan and Laurent Quetton St. George.

What the farmers sold in the market was trifling compared to what they handed over to these merchants. Their entire harvest of wheat, sometimes milled into flour, was destined for the merchants' storehouses. In 1808 one merchant offered his customers who had been in debt for more than a year about seventeen cents for a bushel of wheat; twenty cents a bushel for those who had more current accounts; twenty cents for new customers willing to barter for merchandise in the store; and twenty cents for farmers wanting cash (though instead of cash in hand they received promissory notes due in eight months).

The unlucky and foolish never managed to come out ahead in the credit game. Each year they went deeper into debt and were paid less for their grain. Shopkeepers hiked up their merchandise fifteen percent and charged their customers six percent interest a year. Timothy Nightingale in the summer of 1808 found himself far over his head in debt to Quetton St. George. In May he offered to sell his farm to the merchant:

> As Anderson has disappointed me about taking my farm I am like to disappoint you about the Money due you it is out of my power to pay you unless I sell my farm which is for Sale I have offered to sell for three of four hundred Dollars less than the Value of it but if you know any body that will buy it please to send them and I will take the same that Anderson was to give in order that you may get your pay or I will let you have half of it for twelve Shillings an Acre which is Double what I offer it to you for or I will deliver my farm to you and you may let it out till you get your pay I cant offer anything more if I cant sell and you wont Comply with these terms to gaol I must go.... NB You need not send any officer any more only send a line and I will come up immediately and go to gaol if you say so.

Quetton St. George refused the offer of the farm, and in July Mr. Nightingale was writing again to tell him that he had decided to make potash, the only commodity other than flour that the merchant could readily export:

> I have ben atrying to get money for you to pay you which you know that twice I have ben disopinted I am going to make potash to see if I cant pay you that way if you will Let me alone till I can turn my self to make it part this fall and part in the Spring I shall do my best to pay you I will pay you the Interest of the money from this date you will draw no Interest after Judgment but if you will wate I am willing to pay you then but to spend what I have and then sarten you wont get your pay from your humble sarvent.[1]

Selling in the St. Lawrence Market did not help farmers like the unfortunate Mr. Nightingale. But for others it became progressively more important as the town grew and the tastes of the townspeople became more sophisticated. In their acre garden plots farm women and children were cultivating "red onions, white onions, green marrowfat pease, blood beets, early cabbages, winter cabbages, Savoy cabbages, red cabbages, scarcity, lettuce . . . cranberry beans, early purple beans, asparagus and summer savoury". On a summer Saturday in market square all of this was laid out on trestle tables and heaped into baskets on the ground.

In the early 1830s, as York was being transformed from a town into a city, farmers were coming from greater distances and with more of everything to sell in the market. Many of them could now afford to spend the night in town; Joseph Bloor's hotel on market square, the Farmers' Arms, was the spot where most of them gathered for Friday night refreshments.

A visitor to York in 1831 thought the St. Lawrence Market by far the best stocked and most colourful market he had seen in his entire tour of the province.

> It is astonishing in the time of sleighing in the winter, when the roads are good, to see the number of large sleighs, with

wheat and various kinds of produce coming into town; and it is altogether a very novel sight. Sometimes will be observed fifteen or twenty of those large box sleds, some drawn by two horses, others by four, all at full trot with their bells jingling, some driven by jolly looking Quakers, some by the singular sect called Tankards, who never shave their beards—these growing nearly down to their middles, and with their little skimmer hats and long coats have a most extraordinary appearance. Then comes an Indian, with his well known dress, the universal blanket, driving a load of frozen deer to market,—next a Yankee, with his load of frozen pigs, all as stiff as the shafts of his sleigh, himself dressed in his homespun suit of brown,—all these characters form a very striking contrast. . . . The public market at York is uncommonly well supplied daily with fresh meat, poultry, vegetables, butter, cheese, etc., both in summer and winter. The present market house, which is extensive, appears scarcely large enough to accommodate the inhabitants of this fast increasing town. . . . The price of meat generally in the York market is, for beef about three pence per pound; mutton four pence; veal the same; a fat goose for two shillings; turkeys three and sixpence to five shillings; fowls nine pence to one shilling and six pence; butter eight to ten pence; cheese five pence.[2]

In 1833 the butchers' shambles in the centre of the square were replaced by a "sufficiently neat and commodious brick building of quadrangular shape". A wooden gallery ran around its exterior; underneath were the butchers' stalls. The gallery collapsed in 1834. A high-spirited crowd had gathered there late one July afternoon to hear the city's first mayor, William Lyon Mackenzie, defend his new tax measures. The cheering, catcalling and stamping of feet were too much for the gallery. Five people, mostly Tories, met a grisly fate impaled on the meat hooks in the butchers' stalls below.

The entire front of the building collapsed in the fire of

1849. St. Lawrence Hall was built the following year. Along both sides and down the centre of the hall's hundred-foot-long arcade were stalls for farmers, for hucksters selling toys and perfume, for second-hand book dealers. The butchers occupied most of the space in the new hall. Down one side of the market hung beef and deer, suckling pigs, rabbits and the occasional black bear (which was served up as breakfast steaks in some of the city's better hotels). At the farmers' stalls were huge wild turkeys, sometimes a rare wild swan, plenty of prairie chickens, partridges and grouse.

In the middle of the nineteenth century 25,000 people were living in Toronto. By then they were buying their weekly groceries in five markets. Besides the St. Lawrence there were St. Andrews Market on Little Richmond Street, where meat and vegetables were sold; a small market on the north side of Queen Street, St. Patrick's Market; Wellington Cattle Market; and the hay and wood markets on Front Street. None of them ever rivalled the St. Lawrence Market.

In the last hundred years the St. Lawrence Market has been renovated, rebuilt and refurbished repeatedly, each time to accommodate more vendors and shoppers. In the mid-1970s Toronto's market was expanding into a second, smaller building across the street from market hall. In its 175-year history there were very few years when all the stalls were not rented and all the aisles not jammed with regular customers.

One woman from the city's east end has been shopping in the market for fifty years. "I never go to a supermarket if I can help it. Everything you need is here, at the market. Well, almost everything. Things like milk and toilet paper I go to the supermarket for, of course. But I'm here, bright and early, every Saturday morning. Sometimes when I come, the fruit people haven't got their apples, pears and grapes set out yet. First I usually go around to visit the friends I see every week. You make a lot of friends when you've been

coming fifty years. A few of them have died. The old man I bought apples from, oh, for maybe fifteen years, died quite a while ago. A cheeky old man. A cheeky old farmer. The first time I met him, must have been thirty, thirty-five years ago now, he was yelling out to everyone passing by his stall. I can still hear the old guy. 'Ain't goin' get nothin' better down there. These is the best apples you're goin' find.' Then he'd just go on yelling 'Apples. Apples. Apples.' You could hear him right through the whole market. He was one of those wiry little men, always in overalls. The same pair, I think. Always shining apples with a checkered bandana. I remember him getting really mad at a lady one day. She was picking through one of his baskets, I guess to see if the apples underneath were as good as the ones on top. He didn't like that at all. He took it as an insult. 'Lady, they ain't no different, top or bottom,' he told her, yelling, sort of. The man always yelled. 'I don't cheat nobody. That guy down there he's got bruised apples in the bottom of his baskets. You go buy from him.' That old man must have been ninety years old the last time I saw him. Everybody liked him. He was a real character. Always had time for a chat, though he never stopped shining his apples while we talked. I think he really loved his apples.

"The market is just as good now, you know. Everyone here still has time to talk to you. Pass the time of day, at least. I spend time every week talking to my egg-lady. I think she's been coming here almost as long as me. Maybe longer, I'll have to ask. She's still doing up her own jams and jellies every year. And they're the best you can get anywhere. That lady works hard. She told me one day, not too long ago, that she'd put up a hundred jars that week. And that's besides everything else she does, like tending to her eggs.

"You know, it's not just old folks like me who come here. My children and grandchildren come every week too. I remember the first time I brought my daughter. She must have been four or five then. I had stopped to buy some meat of some kind, and all of a sudden she let out an incredible howl. Made everybody turn around. They thought I was beating her, I guess. It turned into a real tantrum. The butcher I was buying from had about a dozen rabbits hanging up in his stall. Fur and all. Looking a bit bloody besides. Scared the daylights out of her. City kid, you know.

"You see lots of young people, children even, selling things here. Helping their parents and grandparents. It's good for them, working like this. Too many young ones these days don't know what work is. Especially city kids. And the kids selling here are all so polite. Anxious to help and answer questions. They know a lot, too. There's one little boy—a real doll of a lad—knows almost as much about apples as my old apple-man. He's a real charmer.

"You know, the mayor comes here a lot. He's a bit odd, but I voted for him. Maybe because he comes to the market."

# 10 Kitchener Farmers' Market

THE first thing Saturday morning visitors notice about the Kitchener Farmers' Market is the crushing throng. Independent movement would be treacherous were the crowd not so sociable and courteous. The second thing they notice is the smell. Fresh trout, cheddar cheese, kochkäse und kümmel, summer sausage and smoked hams greet the nose before the eye. Coming through the main entrance visitors see fresh, fat buns, mounds of cookies and muffins, shoo-fly pies and, behind the counter, two Mennonite women in organdy prayer caps. Visitors entering through the parking garage, where vendors sell from tables and trucks, encounter bushels and baskets of apples, jars and crocks of dills, sauerkraut and horseradish; the most memorable sight is three jovial gentlemen sipping from wide-mouthed jars something that looks like sauerkraut juice. Upstairs are mostly quiet craftsmen, and the pace slows down long enough to linger over the fancy-work quilts, rag mats, sheepskin mittens and hand-woven jackets, and to eavesdrop on the excited banter of an inventor describing the best apple-corer and cherry-pitter money can buy.

According to many market aficionados, the Kitchener Farmers' Market is the best market in North America and one of the best in the world. On almost every criterion for measuring the success of a market—and certainly on size, fortune and fame—Kitchener's is the best public market in Canada.

Kitchener's market is not as old as many markets in the East, but it seems to have been a prosperous and attractive one almost from the day it was organized. It has had certain advantages from the beginning that others have not. Waterloo County is one of the best agricultural and horticultural areas in the country, and the industrious Mennonites and Germans who have worked the land since the very early years of the nineteenth century have always known the value of a good market to a community of farmers.

The Mennonites began settling Waterloo County at the beginning of the nineteenth century. They were skillful, careful farmers and experienced pioneers. Though they cultivated their first fields with tree-tops and had only beechnuts to feed their pigs in those early years, it was not long before they had surplus grain, hay and livestock to sell. Since their community was still very small and they all had the same things to sell, during their first few decades of settlement they travelled thirty miles to the Dundas market,

*Kitchener Market, c. 1890.*

where their goods were in demand and where they could buy the supplies they needed.

In the early 1830s, after several hundred German immigrants had joined the community and the Millar brothers had opened up the first store in the area, many families began to trade locally. In the Millars' store they bartered butter and eggs for sugar, tea and dry goods. Midway through the 1830s, when there was still no butcher in the small hamlet, farmers notified the community in a newspaper advertisement that on Saturday next they would be bringing carcasses of beef to the store to sell to the first customers showing up at six A.M.

In 1839 Andrew McCullough organized the first public market in the area:

> The Subscriber very respectfully informs his friends and others in Waterloo, that he proposes holding a Market once a Month at the times and places mentioned below, namely: on Wednesday the 4th of September next, at the Mill of Mr. Jacob S. Shoemaker, from 10 o'clock in the forenoon till 3 o'clock in the afternoon—and on Thursday the 5th of September in the Village of Berlin [Kitchener], likewise from 10 a.m. till 3 p.m., which Market is to be continued at the above times and places once a month, the first Wednesday in every month at Mr. Shoemaker's, and the first Thursday in each month in Berlin. At this Farmers' Market, the Subscriber proposes to purchase for cash, the following Country Produce, namely: Cattle and Sheep, Ham, Butter and Eggs. He will also purchase fat Oxen, provided he should find he can realize a small profit from such purchase. It now only remains to invite those Farmers who have any of the said articles for sale, to bring them to his Market, at the times and places mentioned.

By the late 1860s Berlin was sponsoring its own monthly farmers' market. Because of its almost immediate success, several prominent townspeople urged the council to purchase land for a market square. But funds were tight, and most of the town's three thousand residents were tending large home gardens and backyard chickens. Though they rejected the proposed bylaw, in 1869 Reeve Hugo Kranz went ahead and purchased a market site, the same site the Millar brothers had purchased from Bishop Eby in the 1830s for the community's first general store. Mr. Jacob Y. Shantz erected a two-story building on the square for $3,800 to house the council chambers, the market and the telegraph office. In 1872 a long, low market building was erected behind the town hall. For the next twenty-five years Waterloo County farmers crowded into the little market house with their bushels of produce, blocks of well-aged cheese, baskets of eggs and flocks of hissing geese. The market spilled into the square outside on even the coldest and wettest days of the year. Wagons were parked wheel to wheel, some with bleating lambs, squealing sows and wailing calves tethered behind, and others with loads of hay and straw precariously perched on top. In the midst of all this children played rowdy games of tag, screaming and laughing as they raced through the crowd of basket-carrying shoppers and around the old men huddled together for gossip. Black-bonneted grandmothers congregated in another part of the square to watch the babies and compare their grandchildren. Everyone else was buying, selling, haggling over the price of carrots or arguing over the likelihood of rain the next week.

In 1907 a much larger building was erected on the square to contain all this business and chaos. It was a functional, red-brick market house with two stories, a spartan interior and room for four hundred vendors' tables. During their first year in the new market house, vendors sold an average of $7,000 worth of produce every week. The market never faltered. Vendors were always well-supplied and eager to sell, and their customers were just as eager to buy. Even in the bleak 1930s, when money was as scarce as hen's teeth, huge Saturday crowds were typically spending $25,000 in the market. One Kitchener resident remembers both the highpoints and the lowpoints of market days shortly after the Depression:

I recall going to market with my parents and older brother. We went because we needed cash. Desperately. Our family, like most other vendors at the Kitchener farmers' market, was struggling with post-Depression debt. The market was an outlet for the produce of farm wives, and for many the source of income for weekly groceries and family clothing.

Father ran the farm; mother and the kids looked after the market stuff. Except on market days, which were Saturdays from spring to fall. Then the entire family, including fathers, pitched in.

The day began early early—often 4 a.m., sometimes even earlier. We loaded everything into our Model T. Ford. The trunk, the front seat, every nook and cranny were piled high with crates of raspberries, red currants, peas, beans, eggs, chickens, cherries, onions, carrots, whatever was in season and whatever would sell.

By 5:45 we pulled into the market stall, the same place every week, and unloaded the produce and set up our stand. The clients could walk down the concrete promenade. We worked on the pavement at a lower level, looking up anxiously at the picky buyers. It certainly taught farm children early about their relative position in the Canadian mosaic.

While we set up the display, dad would scout the market to check prices. It was a routine that was repeated several times during the morning to make sure we were competitive, a forerunner of the professional Ambler service the supermarkets now pay thousands of dollars to buy to learn about competitors' prices.

In those days, there was a large number of regular weekly shoppers. And the vendors were, of course, the same every week. Friendships and loyalites developed and are maintained to this day. There were no signs here of the farmer-buyer friction, suspicion and jealousies which gave rise to powerful marketing boards.

If, by 1 p.m. when the market closed, we had been unable to sell our entire load of fresh fruits and vegetables, we would sometimes set out to peddle from door to door in modern subdivisions in the Mill Street-Courtland Avenue area and west to Highland Road.

Mom would drive the car, my brother would knock on doors along one side of the street, I along the other. And we would carry samples of our produce—strawberries, raspberries, cherries or whatever. It didn't happen often, but often enough to leave a lasting impression. It had that terrible tinge of begging, and little of the panache and excitement of selling. We priced it cheap and were glad to make a sale, to get rid of the produce so we could get back home and finish up the pressing Saturday work. There was always pressing Saturday work.[1]

The market was housed in the 1907 building for the next sixty-six years. It was here that it gained its reputation as the best market in Canada. In the 1950s and 1960s, when many markets in the country were losing money, customers, vendors and the buildings that housed them, Kitchener's market was thriving. It was attracting out-of-towners with cameras in hand as well as local residents with baskets on their arms. Almost fifteen thousand people passed through the market every Saturday. They all went to the market to buy top quality produce at very reasonable prices, and they also went to enjoy its unique Pennsylvania Dutch charm. Outside, the houses and buggies of the old-order Mennonites were a sightseer's dream. Inside were soft-spoken Mennonite women selling schmearkäse, schwadamahga sausage and apple butter. In those days the Mennonites were the mainstay of the market. And though the fact alarmed them, they were also its biggest attraction.

In 1971 Kitchener city council approved a $15 million

*Photographs here and on the following three pages are of the Waterloo and Kitchener Farmers' Markets.*

downtown redevelopment scheme, which included
demolition of the old market house and city hall and moving
the vendors into larger quarters in the shopping complex
planned for the site. Though the citizens eventually agreed
to the council's scheme in a referendum vote, they were
angered by how far the scheme had progressed in secret
before the public was informed. Few of them worried about
losing the old city hall; most people were more concerned
about how the market would fare in the transition from
market house to shopping complex. On the day the building
met the wrecker's crew, eight thousand residents stood
watching in the rain. Bricks from the old market house sold
that day for a dollar apiece.

Everyone agrees that the new market facilities are
impressive. Wide aisles, modern refrigeration equipment,
space for 430 stalls on two floors inside and another 130
stalls outside, parking space for 750 cars close at hand, an
interior of brick, beams, white-textured wall and
Pennsylvania Dutch folk art, intentionally designed to be
rustic and charming.

Market business has never been better. Stalls are always
fully occupied and always in demand. Eighty-five are rented
by 19 meat vendors; 3 cheese vendors occupy 20 stalls;

chickens, ducks and geese are sold by 4 vendors in 35 stalls;
fish by 2 vendors in 9 stalls; fruit and vegetables by 40
vendors in 120 indoor stalls; and 45 craftsmen and artists in
102 stalls. Another 130 vendors rent produce space outside in
the parking garage.

Vendors pay reasonable rents for their space. Butchers'
stalls rent for $200 a year; indoor produce stalls (each stall is
about 12 square feet) for $35 a year; and outdoor stalls (200
square feet each) for $75 a year. The rates are especially
reasonable in the summer when 25,000 people show up in
the market and leave behind almost $250,000 every
Saturday, and when one egg-lady can sell 4,000 dozen eggs
in 8 hours.

Dealers are not allowed to sell in this market. Even if they
were, it's doubtful they could compete with the market
vendors. The vendors in the Kitchener Farmers' Market are
professional sellers. They know the value of large,
picturesque signs displaying at least two of five or so
favourite catchwords—"organically grown", "fresh-picked",
"homemade", home-grown" and "farm-fresh"; how to turn a
heap of lettuce and onions into a tempting tableau; how to
pass the time of day with each customer while quickly
wrapping up a package of pigs' tails; how to haggle for ten

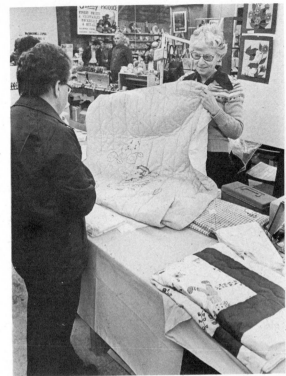

minutes without budging a penny; and how to entice customers into buying an extra pound or two and send them away happy to have bought more for less. All the wonderful sights, sounds and smells succeed in producing their calculated effect. Consumers are helpless to resist as soon as they enter the market and are confronted by fresh, homemade pecan pies, farm-fresh eggs and fresh-picked, organically grown sweet corn.

The market is understandably one of the city's chief tourist attractions. Busloads of visitors from all over Canada, the United States and Britain, as well as from just about everywhere else, troop through the market and line up at the stall selling souvenirs: calico aprons like those worn by Mennonite women, dolls dressed in old-order Mennonite costumes, histories of the local Mennonite community, and cookbooks of recipes for traditional Mennonite dishes.

Ironically, most of the old-order Mennonites withdrew as vendors when the market moved into the shopping complex in 1974. Though they were once the market's foundation and certainly the reason for its success, there are now only a few Mennonites still selling in the market. The others have moved to the Elmira and Waterloo markets, both of which closely resemble the Kitchener market of the old days— spartan and functional facilities, selling in the open air and shoppers who come to buy food rather than be entertained. Many of their regular customers followed them.

There are a few vendors in the Kitchener Farmers' Market who regret the changes of the last six years. According to one who sold produce in the old market house for forty years: "It's not the same as the old market. All the Mennonites are gone, for one thing. And in the old market house we didn't have all these crafts here. We sold food—that's what a market's for. I sort of liked the old market better. I was more comfortable there in some ways. I knew everybody and had known them all for years. It seems to me that everybody, at least all the vendors, used to go to that market because they loved it. We sure had some grand times there. Sometimes now I think everybody just comes here to make lots of money. And there's no doubt a lot of them do. But I don't like to complain too much about this new building. It sure is warmer in here in the winter."

# 11 Markets in Winnipeg

TOO much. Too much. Can't afford to eat 'em, for what you're askin'."

"Go way. Go way. Too busy. You only complain. Too busy."

"You ain't goin' sell cabbages for that price. You'll have to take 'em all home."

"No time for crazy man. Half dollar each. I sell half dollar each."

"To much. Too much."

"You want 'em? Half dollar each."

"Lady. I'm only goin' eat 'em."

"Worth more. Sell 'em cheap. Best here."

"Come on. They're not that good. I've had lots better. I'm not payin' a half dollar each."

"Go 'way. No time."

"Tell you what. Two heads and a bunch of carrots. One dollar."

"You crazy. Carrots half dollar."

"Two heads and four cukes. One dollar."

"One dollar half."

"Here's a dollar. One head. And two bunches of carrots."

"You rob me. Two big heads. Dollar."

"You're a hard, hard lady. O.K. Those two heads there."

"O.K. You come next week?"

There is no other market in Canada quite like Winnipeg's Northend Farmers' Market. It sits in the middle of a neighbourhood that was created during the city's boom years mainly by Slavic, Jewish, German and Scandinavian immigrants. The Old World traditions and customs they brought with them have given the community its special character, one that is lively and tenacious. At least this is what emerges in their dealings with each other in the market. Only in this market is the venerable art of haggling still practiced, and with such shrewd skill. None of the vendors posts a list of his prices. Carrots, cucumbers and jars of dills are passed from seller to buyer only after a bit of back-and-forth bantering. (Some of them call it yattering.)

Many of these people have been haggling with each other for forty years, from the time the market was first set up. A market-gardening family leased the space on Main Street in 1938. Some of the twenty or so vendors now operating have been occupying the same spot ever since. There are no elaborate facilities. Vendors sell from the backs of their

trucks, from card tables and overturned crates. Customers bring their own baskets and shopping bags into which lettuce, onions and cauliflower are dumped in a jumble.

Nothing moves very quickly here. A pound of beans is selected, bean by bean. A bunch of radishes is discarded for another because one radish looks woody. The number of dills in a jar are counted and compared with those in the jars at the next table. Customers step over and around others bent over crates of pickling cucumbers. No one buys anything without first checking out who has the best goods and who looks most likely to drive an easy bargain.

"You know, I've been bringing stuff to this market for a long time and I can't see that it's changed much in the last twenty years. Except we're all older. Not too many young people interested in selling in the market anymore. Don't know what's going to happen when we all die off. Guess it'll just close down. Not too many young people even interested in farming anymore. Lots of farms for sale where I come from. Old people can't keep up with the work and their kids are gone off to the city. Can't blame them too much. It's tough being a farmer if you only got a small farm. Oh, there's lots of big ones. Big machines. But that's not farming,

that's business. Big business. Government sure don't help the small farmer. The real problem is those marketing boards. Sure they looked good in the beginning. They were supposed to help all us small people, but then they got to be big business too. They help the big farmer now. Only place we small farmers can sell our stuff is in places like this. In the markets. I don't make a lot of money here. But enough. On a day like this, maybe $150 for the truckload. Sometimes more, sometimes less. I just like coming here, guess that's the reason. I don't need to come, you know. I just like talking to the people. Seeing how all my friends are. You see mostly the same customers every Saturday. They all live around here. I see maybe two or three faces I don't recognize. See that white-haired lady, all dressed up? Looks a bit uncomfortable, doesn't she? Sightseeing, I guess. Don't get too much of that. Most city people don't even know we're here. No, everybody knows everybody in this market. Vendors and customers. Most of my customers are regulars. Lots of times I take orders from them one week and bring in what they want the next. I sell most of my potatoes that way. People here don't buy their potatoes ten pounds at a time, like the people who shop in supermarkets. They buy in bulk, especially things like potatoes and carrots. Sell a lot of fifty-pound bags of carrots. The customers are particular. Really particular. They know quality when they see it. Not like most people nowadays. They're getting better food here all round. You know those potatoes they're selling in the supermarkets? They're full of chemicals. A farmer who's got two hundred acres of potatoes isn't going to take chances. So he uses every darn chemical he can get his hands on. There's nothing in my potatoes but potatoes. It's the same for everyone selling here. None of us use chemicals. People don't know sometimes what a good deal they're getting here. I mean quality mostly. None of us sell too cheap. We got to make a living too. But we sell reasonable. Some people are real stupid about farmers. People from the city especially. Think they're going to come here and get things dirt cheap from us. I had one lady from the city—her first time here— who got mad because she'd come all the way here for tomatoes expecting them to be half the price she's paying in the supermarket. I was asking the wholesale price for them. And they were beautiful tomatoes. Just picked that morning. Fat and juicy. Not like those big marbles they sell in the supermarkets. They're picked almost green. You know, they now have a kind of tomato that's square-shaped, just to make it easier to truck them. The people that did that don't care what they taste like. Or what they look like. Just so they don't get squashed in the truck. I don't like it. What's happening to our food, I mean. We need a lot more markets like this one so people can buy good food right from the farmer. It's the only way customers can find out what they're really getting. At least they can ask the farmer what kind of chemicals he's used. He's probably not used any, but at least they can be sure that way. You don't see all those chemicals listed on the bags of potatoes you buy in the supermarket. No, we sure need more markets. But I bet the city people wouldn't use them. They're not like the people here in the Northend. Sometimes I think they're not as smart. There's

116 TO MARKET, TO MARKET

supposed to be a new market where the old city market used to be. Haven't been there myself, but someone was telling me the other day that he'd been there. He didn't like it much. He says it's the kind of market that city people who've never been in a market would set up. He says they sell mostly flowers and knickknacks. Some fish, some vegetables. There are a few farmers there, I guess. No, no one ever asked us to sell our stuff there. Wouldn't go anyway. My friend says it's mostly for tourists. And for people who need something to do on Saturday and Sunday. Says it's pretty down there, though. No, I'll stay here with my regular customers. I'd probably feel silly down there anyway. I like the Northend. This is a real market."

There is a new market on Old Market Square. The colourfully-canopied outdoor market was organized by the Old Market Square Association, a group of businessmen in the area who wanted to provide the downtown with "a people place", at least on the weekends. About thirty vendors show up each Saturday morning. A few with B.C. salmon. A few more with fresh produce. Some with homemade soup of the ethnic variety. Some with antiques and trinkets. Many with flowers and potted plants. Others with candles and sandlewood soap, jewelry, pottery and junk. Occasionally there's a strolling minstrel. Sometimes a card-reader and palmist.

It seems to be a popular spot for city people. "This is just what Winnipeg needs. A real market. Someplace where we can get fresh fruits and vegetables. There's no place else in the city where you can get fresh produce like this. And it's fun coming here. I guess I come down at least once or twice a month. Mostly just for fun. I buy a few tomatoes when I can, sometimes a bit of fruit. I really just come down for the entertainment."

One old gentleman had a very different view of

Winnipeg's newest market. "This isn't a market. Not a real market. Not with all that stuff over there. Those silly little trinkets. They don't belong in a real market. A market is for selling food. A market's supposed to have farmers. You don't for a minute think those people over there grew those cucumbers. Hell, they bought them from a wholesaler probably. Oh, maybe some of them grow their own. But not many. I remember the old market. The one that used to be here. City tore it down about twenty years ago. Now that was a market. And it was full of farmers. Always full of farmers. And lots of butchers, too. I remember those butchers' stalls. Seemed like there was sawdust a foot deep in those stalls. There was one old lady in there—at least she seemed old to me, I was just a kid then—who came every week with dozens and dozens and dozens of eggs. I'd like to have seen just how many chickens she had. Seemed like it must have been thousands. She just kept bringing those eggs week after week. Oh, she sold other things too. Big rounds of cheese, I remember. But she was mostly an egg-lady. I bet she got rich selling those eggs. I loved going to the market as a kid. I went every week with my mother. She bought everything there. Well, maybe not flour and sugar. We got that at the store. But mostly everything else we ate came from that market. She made the rounds every time but she usually ended up buying from the same people week after week. There was one lady who sold her own sausages. She always gave my mother a quarter pound extra because she was such a good customer. Every fall we bought three hundred pounds of potatoes from this old farmer. A real mean-looking man. At least he looked mean to me. Always wore a hat pulled down low on his head. Never smiled. Shouted when he talked. He didn't talk much, though. He had a farm about twenty miles north of here. He was still hauling his potatoes to market in a wagon when everyone else was driving a truck. That must have been a long trip. Maybe that's why he looked so mean. He was tired before he started."

# 12 Markets in Saskatchewan

ONCE Saskatchewan had left its pioneering days behind and individual self-sufficiency had given way to community self-sufficiency, public markets appeared in Regina, Prince Albert, Saskatoon and a few other rapidly-growing villages and towns. The markets did their duty for local trade and then disappeared. Prince Albert boarded up its market in 1922, and Regina's closed down a few years later.

Saskatchewan has very few fruit and vegetable growers. Farm enterprise in the province is not geared to cabbages and pumpkins; capital and labour are tied up in thousand-acre spreads and 200 horsepower tractors. Cabbages and pumpkins are not even a sideline. Eighty percent of the province's fruits and vegetables—the staples of a farmers' market—are imported.

In 1974 a pilot project launched by the Saskatchewan Department of Agriculture changed the province's attitude toward farmers' markets. With the help of the department, four markets were established and closely watched during the first year. The response from both producers and consumers was overwhelmingly positive. The following year the Saskatchewan Farmers' Market Program was instituted and in the spring six markets opened for business—in Regina,

Saskatoon, Prince Albert, Yorkminster, Battleford and Lloydminster. In 1976 the Prince Albert market already had 46 vendors selling locally-grown fruits and vegetables. Its only worry on market days was "crowd control".[1] By 1978 there were 350 producers and 150,000 consumers involved in 7 markets, and the annual combined sales figure was approaching $350,000.

Without the initiative, financial support and advice of the provincial Department of Agriculture, there would probably not be a single new farmers' market in Saskatchewan. Setting up a new market is formidable enough in an area that already has a strong market tradition; it is much more difficult in a province that has had little experience either in growing the staples or in marketing them directly. In order for a market to be even minimally successful, several basic criteria have to be met. There should be at least a dozen producers supplying a variety of high-quality goods including fruits, vegetables, eggs, flowers and meat. These producers must be able to reach the market in less than three hours; a round trip of no more than a hundred miles is considered optimal. Surveys have indicated that few consumers will travel more than six miles to shop in a market, which means that within that distance there must be three (preferably

122  TO MARKET, TO MARKET

*Vegetable vendors from two Saskatchewan Hutterite colonies.*

five) thousand consumers willing to change their buying habits and switch their allegiance from supermarket to farmers' market. Adequate facilities have to be available; the rent charged to vendors must be reasonable; and parking space must be close at hand. It's a tall order, and probably an impossible one to fill without the assistance of the provincial government.

Saskatchewan's Department of Agriculture offers a $1,000 renewable grant for new markets and another $1,200 stipend for promotion and advertising. To receive the initial grant, a market must be a co-operative, consisting of at least three local producers and a regional co-ordinator appointed by the ministry. More than half the vendors must be either farmers or market gardeners, and all vendors must be either Saskatchewan producers or craftsmen. The Saskatchewan government spends about $60,000 a year on its Farmers' Market Program. But it is considered money well spent if producers are encouraged to take advantage of this alternative source of income, and consumers are weaned from imported fruits and vegetables.

While the ministry shoulders the responsibility of supervising all farmers' markets in the province, each individual market succeeds or fails on the basis of community support and involvement. Thus far, all signs indicate that the program is a big success. After the novelty had worn off, vendors and shoppers were still enthusiastic and eager to maintain the momentum. Farmers' markets now seem to be a secure feature of Saskatchewan's agricultural community.

# 13 Edmonton City Market

IT was 1901 before Edmonton began worrying about a public market. Despite its late start—about 150 years after Halifax—it soon found itself dealing with the same kinds of problems.

Edmonton began as a fur-trading post in 1795. For the next hundred years the only trading of basic necessities carried on was the exchange of pemmican and fresh buffalo meat for tobacco, tools and brandy. It was straight barter which occasionally grew complicated: "At 5 PM two young Indians arrived for Tobacco and Powder and also Brandy, the former they got but the latter I could not give without I had given the whole Keg such as it was, not being master of one small [one] to Distribute Brandy in. . . . It must be a silly notion to send Strong Liquor Inland without a Cooper to make small Kegs to divide it in, it is well known that natives have no Kegs of their own."[1]

Other food for the fur-traders' table came from the Edmonton House farm. It had a slow and very modest beginning. In 1810 one of the post's staff was sent out to plant turnips and radishes in the woods. A year later the word went around that Fort Edmonton's hens were finally laying. Eventually the farm was producing small crops of barley and oats and bushels and bushels of potatoes.

The traders' diet was fairly monotonous most of the time, but when the occasion called for it they could put on a splendid feast. Like the famous Christmas dinner Paul Kane shared with them in 1846:

> At the head, before Mr. Harriett was a large dish of boiled buffalo-rump; at the foot smoked a boiled buffalo calf. Start not, gentle reader, the calf is very small, and is taken from the cow by the Caesarian operation long before it attains its full growth. This boiled whole is one of the most esteemed dishes amongst the epicures of the interior. My pleasing duty was to help a dish of mouffle, or dried moose nose; the gentleman on my left distributed, with graceful impartiality, the white fish, delicately browned in buffalo marrow. The worthy priest helped the buffalo tongue, whilst Mr. Rundell cut up the beavers' tails. Nor was the other gentleman left unemployed, as all his spare time was occupied in dissecting a roast wild goose. The centre of the table was graced with piles of potatoes, turnips and bread conveniently placed so that each could help himself without interrupting the labour of his companions. Such was our jolly Christmas dinner at Edmonton; and long will it remain in my memory, although no pies, or puddings, or blanc manges shed their fragrance over the scene.[2]

By the late 1850s the farm had thirty acres planted, mostly in barley and potatoes. When the farm's potato crop failed, the community's meat supply was rationed. The 150 people connected with the post were restricted to six pounds of buffalo meat each per day. Wheat-growing was out of the question. The familiar varieties needed at least 135 days to ripen, far too long for this land of early frosts. The farm's flour supply came from the Red River and from as far away as England.

In the late 1880s Edmonton began to look more like a town. And for the first time it was attracting settlers eager to farm. "There were six mercantile establishments whose stock consisted of every imaginable thing from sides of bacon to ostrich plumes," an early townsmen recalled. "There was also a butcher-shop, a baker's, a blacksmith shop, a land office, the *Edmonton Bulletin* printing-establishment, and a carriage-maker's shop, four churches, two schools, four hotels, a post office, telegraph office, grist-mill, saw-mill and a brick-yard. Small settlements of homesteaders at Namao, Belmont, Stony Plain, Clover Bar, and eastward at Beaver Lake, gave to the little village its promise of a widening agricultural industry to take the place of a receding fur-trade."

The community was still too small and the villagers too self-sufficient to need a market. Any exchanging of necessities was between merchants and farmers. They would cart six crocks of butter into a general merchant's shop to establish credit, haul away sixty dollars worth of supplies and return after harvest to settle the bill and start a new account. The kinds of things the farmers had to sell the townspeople didn't yet need; they were themselves producing most of what ended up on their family's table.

Everybody had their own cow and there was this sort of a town pasture. . . . It was where everybody put their cows. It had a wooden fence around it and you paid the helper at the livery barn I think about 50 cents a week, and it was his job to take the cows to the pasture and bring them home for evening milking.

It was up to you to see that the cow was tied up outside your house in the morning so the hosteler could pick it up, and it was your job in the evening to get it when the herd came through town. You did this by the bell. Every cow had a different kind of bell. Some would go clink, some would go clank, one would go thunk, another would tinkle, and you'd hear your bell coming with the herd, and you'd go out and there would be your cow. . . . She'd go around the side of the

*Edmonton market scenes,* left ro right: *Market Square, 1905; city market, c.1920; before 1929; c.1930.*

house, her old bag swaying, and whoever did the milking would get out the stool and away you'd go. That was the way you got your milk.[3]

In the early 1890s, though the farmers were producing enough wheat to keep several mills operating, the town's merchants and the Hudson's Bay Company were still handling most of the food trade. In 1893 the Company sold a ton of butter it imported from Manitoba, and one resourceful butcher brought in from Ontario more than a ton of turkeys and geese for Christmas.

When Edmonton incorporated as a town in 1892, its population stood at seven hundred. By the turn of the century the new settlers taking up homesteads in the area and the new shopkeepers and businessmen who came to supply them and the greenhorns heading for the Yukon goldfields had added another two thousand people. There were finally enough townspeople too busy to worry about collecting cows from the hosteler and enough farmers with surplus produce to sell to set up a public market.

In 1901 the town council of Edmonton passed a bylaw to raise $4,000 for purchasing land for a market site. Two weeks later the bylaw was "submitted to the burgesses and approved". Nine lots "for the purpose of a public market"

were immediately acquired from Mrs. Isabella Heiminck for $3,500, and another two from Henri Morel for $700. In 1905 the city council passed another bylaw to raise $40,000 to buy more land for the market. It was also "submitted to the burgesses and approved", as was the 1909 bylaw to raise $45,000 for a market site.

As the council got deeper and deeper into the market scheme, the country vendors went happily about their business selling directly from the wagons and carts they parked wheel-to-wheel in market square. In 1910 the city had almost twenty thousand people to feed, and farmers willingly came in from settlements as far as sixty miles away. What attracted them was cash, as one butter-and-egg man put it. "We want to sell dear and buy cheap. We prefer to go to a town or city where we can sell for cash. We will very likely spend the cash again in the same town. But we will come to the town to trade where we can sell for cash."

Edmonton's council had been promising a market house for almost a decade. Though the farmers did not seem to mind its procrastination, one citizen certainly did.

The market building is to remain a castle in the air for another year. . . . In time the project will become a perpetual

heritage for succeeding councils and be handed down from generation to generation as one of the venerable and venerated traditions of the City. In prospect of this it is humbly suggested that the plans and specifications for the building be enclosed in the hollow end of a baseball bat and this good stick, fitly gilded and ornamented be laid upon the table of the civic parliament. . . . By all means let us have the plans enshrined in the mace, that when future aldermen gaze upon this gilded bauble they may feel that they are free to do as they please even after they have asked the people what to do and have been told in the plainest of terms.

What this writer for the *Bulletin* forgot to mention was that the city was operating its two markets—the produce market on Rice Street and the hay market on First Street—at a loss of more than $2,000. "In the hope of changing a loss into a revenue" the city turned over the market privilege to private hands. Mr. Kelly and Mr. Ennes paid the city $2,020 and agreed to keep both markets operating, to maintain the weigh scales in good repair and to weigh all goods coming into the market.

In the process of handing over the market, the city changed some of the rules. No cattle or horses hereafter could be fed at the Rice Street market. No meat was to be cut up at either market, and no hucksters could sell in the markets before noon. The weighing fees went up. A farmer was charged a dime for weighing a load over five thousand pounds and a nickel for "live animals on foot" if he had more than two. Otherwise it was a dime. One new rule—charging the farmers a dime a day for use of the market—would cause a miniature riot.

Until then the country vendors had been a rather placid lot, satisfied with their cash receipts in the market, making no demands for a roof over their heads. The new market fee brought out a different character entirely. All the farmers complained about the dime. Three flatly refused to pay and

*A Hutterite vendor in Calgary.*

left in a huff. Another agreed to pay at the outset but later tried to rush the gate. "The gatekeeper was, however, guarding the exit and the farmer had to turn over the cash besides his name and address." The city held its own in the riot. "Some of the farmers think they are running the market," one alderman argued. "They have had things their own way for some years and now kick when the city simply enacts rules to permit the proper administration of the market. . . . The city is not anxious to make money out of the market, but simply to pay expenses, while the farmers think they should get it free."

In 1912 the city, again in control of the markets and now somewhat more cautious, finally built the long-awaited Rice Street market house. The vendors paid their dimes a little less reluctantly. A year later Edmonton voted in a new mayor. He must not have been involved in the earlier fracas because he boldly moved the vendors to a new location (at the corner of 101 Street and 107 Avenue). It was not a good move. Customers complained about the long hike to the new site, and the vendors complained even louder. Within a year they were back selling in market square. There they stayed until the early 1960s when the civic centre took over the square. The demolished market building had accommodated 141 small stalls and more than seventy larger spaces for greenhouse operators. One eighty-eight-year-old lady had been selling her eggs and poultry there since 1916. Another poulterer from Leduc was forced to relinquish the stall his family had rented in 1913.

Despite its late start and numerous fumbles, Edmonton now operates a fine public market. The only current problem seems to be parking. The forty-eight vendors are among the most fastidious in the country. There is non-stop rearranging of honey pails, crocheted doilies and embroidered aprons; half-hourly mistings of gladioli and mums; and slightly less regular dousings of carrots and cabbages.

Edmonton also has some of the best market hawkers in the country. "Fresh romaine, Boston or bib!" is trumpeted from a corner. "Fresh Hawaiian Vegetables by Air" blares a sign up front. "Homegrown, organic beets and broccoli, freshly picked" is occasionally audible over "Get your brown eggs here, cheap and still warm from the nest." The lapidary lady sells her polished rock jewelry simply by being charming. The garlic, onions, dill and mint sell themselves by sending their lively scents through the market.

With a nod to its riotous past, the Edmonton City Market is also the only market in Canada that employs a full-time bouncer.

Left: *A Hutterite father and son sell vegetables in Calgary.* Below: *A market in Medicine Hat.*

# 14 Markets in Vancouver

VANCOUVER has never been a comfortable place for public markets. The first city market lasted only a decade. Market Hall was built on the corner of Main and Pender in 1889. On market days pigs were sold outside, cows in the basement, and chickens and vegetables on the main floor. Meanwhile the public hall upstairs was often being outfitted for a fancy-dress ball or a travelling farce. In 1896 City Hall moved upstairs and two years later all the chickens and cows and farmers moved out.

The odds were against Market Hall from the beginning. A year after it opened, buyers and sellers everywhere in the city floundered in the midst of a depression. It hurt the market far more than the city's retail establishments. Most grocers survived the worst times by offering their customers credit. In the market customers had to pay cash for their butter and eggs; farmers selling there needed cash to pay off their own debts to the shopkeepers. So most people bought their butter and eggs from grocers on credit rather than from vendors in the market. When the market closed, there was genuine surprise in some quarters that it had not closed sooner.

After Market Hall became City Hall some farmers became pedlars. They did not like peddling much. "This doesn't do me any good bringing my potatoes here. Wears out the horse, that's all. I've sold maybe a hundred pounds of potatoes today, and that wasn't easy either. They make you feel like you were begging them to buy your potatoes. No amount of smiling or talking up to them is going to change that. It's degrading. Yes, that's what it is, degrading."

One seasoned huckster, who made a living buying from farmers and wholesalers and selling door to door, looked at the peddling business somewhat differently. "Those farmers, they don't know what they're doing. They come to the city, two, three times a month at best, with a wagonload of eggs or turnips or potatoes and they just expect everyone to come running. When they stop at a house they don't even know enough to go to the back door sometimes. And when they bang on someone's door they start right off with 'You want some potatoes?' Now I have regular customers, and they're glad to see me. I know I've got at least a hundred ladies every week waiting for my eggs. They know me and I know them. That's what makes the difference."

City people who bought on credit from grocers and had their eggs and butter deposited on their doorsteps by professional pedlars did not need a market. And farmers eventually found alternative ways of selling their surplus

*The public market is the centrepiece of the Granville Island renewal project designed by Norman Hotson Architects. Photographs by Yvonne Grue.*

produce. Some of them made weekly trips to the market at New Westminster, some sold to pedlars and wholesalers, others to shopkeepers in the city. Both consumers and farmers soon developed stronger habits of private dealing than of public marketing.

Most of those habits are still active and intact. Many food pedlars now buy fruits and vegetables from farmers and wholesalers to resell to consumers from the back of trucks parked at strategic locations on the major highways outside the city. Some of them sell to neighbourhood "ma and pa stores", acting as small-time wholesalers rather than as retailers. Though as popular as ever with consumers, they are vigorously disliked by other members involved in the food trade, especially by marketing boards. They are accused of having an unfair advantage over wholesalers and retailers because they seldom bother with things like licences (and income tax) and can pick up and go wherever business is better.

The truck pedlars are in more direct competition with roadside retailers. British Columbia has about two hundred commercially operated roadside stands and two hundred more that belong to fruit and vegetable growers. Ten out of every hundred apples sold in the province pass through these stands. Families who operate their own stands pay no licensing fee, cart their produce no further than the end of their driveways, are bothered by few restrictions and usually succeed in pocketing more cash than they would competing with other vendors in a public market.

Food pedlars for years and roadside stands since at least the 1950s have eliminated the need for public markets. Both supply Vancouver consumers with fresh products from the farm. And the roadside stands give them a chance to deal face-to-face with farmers, which has traditionally been the one clear advantage of the market.

Undaunted by their lack of a market tradition and of

experience in public marketing, Vancouverites in the mid-1970s decided they wanted a public market. Unfortunately, their enthusiasm for the idea of a market did not seem to be matched by a thorough understanding of what was entailed in setting one up and keeping it operating.

A farmer's-fisherman's market opened at the foot of Columbia Street in 1977. It is typically referred to as the "troubled Gastown Market". In the beginning everything about the market was wonderful. People who had claimed they would come to a market if the city gave them one arrived in full force. A dozen or so farmers trucked in eggplants and raspberries; fishermen laid out shiny, bright-eyed salmon on tables of ice. The market was charming and colourful, noisy and gregarious, just as a market should be. Two months later most of the activity and ambience had disappeared. During the week farmers sat around watching their ripe tomatoes perish and talking to restless fishmongers anxious to get back to their boats. When some farmers moved out of the market, a few reliable old food pedlars happily took their places.

Parking had always been a problem and the facilities inadequate and shaky. Little was done to entice shoppers to the market, and when the novelty was gone, few came on their own. They were still falling back on their old habits of buying food from supermarkets, from pedlars and roadside stands. Not much was left of the Gastown Market two years after it began.

Enthusiasm and scepticism were running almost neck and neck when Granville Island Public Market opened in July 1979. Enthusiasm had the edge because Vancouverites suddenly found themselves with "the largest and most beautiful market building in the country".

The old Island home of B.C. Equipment has been imaginatively rejuvenated to house a 46,000-square-foot marketplace, with an exposed skeleton of timber beams, cedar poles and industrial fixtures, and with enough skylights

PUMPERNIXOL ONION    POPPY

and overhead windows to lift the dullest spirits. Inside is an assortment of shops and stalls for retailers and producers, mostly for producers.

When they trek out to the new market, Vancouver consumers find fishmongers filleting red snappers, a white-aproned butcher weighing fresh lamb chops, country people unloading crates of cucumbers, broccoli, cauliflowers and pears, a baker unpacking fresh buns, a fish-and-chip vendor, a few craftsmen, flower-sellers, a retailer displaying shiny pots and slotted spoons, a Kwik Save shopkeeper and a souvlaki-vendor.

Most Vancouver people are torn between shopping and sightseeing when they visit the market. "This building is magnificent. I felt cheered up and energetic as soon as I walked in. Everything and everyone cheers you up here. I talked to a lady selling spinach and broccoli and cucumbers. At least that's all she had left when I stopped. We talked about the weather, about the market, mostly about cucumbers. Next week she's bringing me a basket of those long, skinny ones that are just the right size for bread-and-butters. I didn't buy much today. I came mostly to look. But next week I'm bringing my kids to help me carry everything."

The lady selling the long, skinny cucumbers was pleased when her day was over. "I'm tired now. It's been a long day. I was up at six and in the garden picking. I've been here since eight. There's lots of unpacking to do right off, setting things up so they look nice. But I'm not complaining, mind you. Everything's gone, except for a few cauliflowers. I was worried a bit when the market first opened that no one would come. That's happened before, at the Gastown Market. Not worried about that anymore. I've already got lots of steady customers who stop by at least once a week. I've still got my fingers crossed, though."

The sceptics, who had winced at all the hoopla

surrounding the opening of the Island market, were eventually reassured. The crowds never dwindled from a "steady stream during the week and a happy torrent on the weekends". After six months people came mostly to shop and only a little to admire their exciting new marketplace. Some vendors experienced shortages three hours into the market day. Business was good for most of them and looked like it would get progressively better. Some Vancouverites are now boldly throwing caution to the winds and predicting that the Island market will survive.

A great deal of care has been taken to ensure its survival. A lot more than "wouldn't it be nice to have a market" has gone into setting up this one. The marketplace is the centrepiece of the Granville Island Redevelopment Plan, which is an open-ended (and federally-funded) project aimed at creating an old-style community on the Island.

For the Island planners and schemers the marketplace is more important than the market; the social and cultural aspects of the market tradition more important than the economic ones. They want a place where people gather to exchange not only life's necessities but ideas and skills and neighbourly gossip. A place full of diverse interests. The traditional rules and regulations that have been protecting diverse interests in public markets since the Middle Ages are being followed in the Island marketplace. Few middlemen are allowed space in the market. It is intended primarily for small-scale farmers, gardeners and craftsmen. Like market town officials in the Middle Ages, the Island planners aim at bringing many buyers and sellers together.

The decision to establish a marketplace rather than simply a public market was a wise one. It has been clear since Market Hall disappeared in 1898 that Vancouver does not really need a public market where people congregate only to buy and sell fresh fruits and vegetables. Food pedlars and roadside retailers cornered that market a long time ago.

# 15 Markets in Victoria

**V**ICTORIA has not had a public market since 1959. But the city has had the most tempestuous and well-recorded market history in the country.

It all started in 1861. A group of private businessmen, anxious to see their town acquire all the amenities of civilization, formed the Victoria Market Company and built a large and handsome market house on Fort Street. It was more than handsome, according to the editor of the *Colonist*: "No city on the coast can boast of a finer market building." The editor had already told his readers what a wonderful thing this new market would be:

> We have no doubt but the establishment of this market will prove a great public convenience, as well as a considerable saving to farmers. The latter now labor under serious disadvantage in this city, being compelled to hawk their commodity from door to door, sell what they can (in quantities to suit), and either take the balance back home or dispose of it at a sacrifice to the produce dealers. If the proposed market only affords this class relief we shall be most happy to give this project our cordial support.

Markets do not thrive on cordial support, as the editor soon discovered. Less than six months after it opened, the market building was auctioned off to the highest bidder.

Twenty years later, when the editor was vigorously pressing for a new city market, he recalled this first attempt as a scheme that failed because "there were scarcely any farmers and hardly any home-grown produce".

The market house went for $750, and everybody wondered about its fate. The editor was happy to announce in his column a month after its sale that

> the momentous question "what is to be done with the Victoria Market property?" has been settled at last. Yesterday we observed a number of carpenters at work siding up the half-dozen stalls, and on inquiring the object, were informed that they were building a dance-hall. That settles the question at last, and we are glad of it. Half the people in town have been racking their brains over it for a month past. . . . Some said it would make a fine lunatic asylum in which to confine the persons holding shares in it. But . . . Madam Terpsichore has hired the building herself at $15 a month rent.

In 1862 some marketing was going on in the old quarters, as our editor casually discovered one day:

> Passing along Fort Street yesterday we heard a suspicious noise issuing from the enclosure of the market grounds, and on entering discovered that three of the stalls were occupied

as poultry stands. This is doing pretty well. Nine of the stalls are now leased—three for the sale of poultry and six for the sale of something else. The institution is looking up.

It died six months later.

In 1867 Victorians were convinced the time had come for a public market and wrote letter after letter to the editor of the *Colonist* describing in detail the need for such an institution.

You have several times urged in your columns the necessity of a public market. Those who buy as well as those who raise produce suffer much for want of this. Indeed, it is surprising that such a market has not been established long ere this. Those who bring to town the produce of their gardens get scarcely more than pays its carriage thither; those who bring cattle find that they eat their heads off before sold; and those who arrive with a season's prime pork from Comox or Cowichan have to hawk it round the town till disgusted with the whole concern. Now this is not for want of buyers, but because buyers and sellers are not brought together. For instance, I met a farmer who had been peddling round with 1,000 lbs. of new potatoes, which he had pulled up in his boat under a sweltering sun. He did not wish to pull them back and offered them at any price. The same evening I met a gentleman who was victualling a ship about to sail, and who that very day had been hunting around for 1,000 lbs of new potatoes, and offering much more than the other sought. As it was in the beginning of the season, no one had so large a stock and he had considerable difficulty in making up the supply in small quantities. . . . Indeed we want a market and want it badly. Do help us Mr. Editor.

Help came first from Mr. J. P. Davies who in 1868 set aside part of his cattle sale yard for this badly needed market. To the editor of the *Colonist*, he wrote:

Having seen the necessity of a public market mooted for some time past, whereby farmers and others can have a place to sell their produce on stated days, and as no action has been taken on this matter, we propose to open the Cattle Sale Yard every Saturday (or more frequently) from 7 a.m. to 12 o'clock noon, for the sale of such produce as may be offered, such as fruits, grain, hay, straw, butter, eggs, cheese, or poultry, rabbits, goats, pigs, sheep, horses, mules, cattle of every description, etc., etc., etc. The charges are to be within the reach of everyone.

Mr. Davies's ambitious undertaking was not, unfortunately, a success. Six months after he had offered Victorians a marketplace, they were busy writing letters to the *Colonist* editor, trying again to engage his influential support for "a proper public market".

I will simply mention the benefit which would accrue both to producer and consumer: the former, instead of carrying around to various stores, grain, vegetables, etc., which he is obliged to sell at whatever price may be offered rather than return home with his cart full, will take them direct to the market where he will be brought into immediate contact with the consumer, who will at all times give the fair and proper price in cash. The latter will, to the great benefit of his family, be able at all times to obtain fresh vegetables, eggs, butter, etc., at the lowest price. As the father of a family I can testify to the difficulty I have in obtaining these articles, and to the regret which I felt at being obliged to be dependent on the occasional visits of a Chinaman.

Late in 1868 the editor announced that it looked as if the city would finally have its public market: "A number of influential and thoroughly business gentlemen are exerting themselves to reestablish our public market—a great benefit to all classes, but at the same time a self-sustaining institution." No market appeared.

By 1872 the editor was leading the fight for a market and arousing citizens to join him. A public meeting, attended mostly by farmers, passed a resolution to request that the

Facing p.151 and left: *Scenes from Victoria marketplace, c.1930.*

city's mayor set up a public meeting to discuss the "feasibility of a public market". In December the Farmers Club proposed that forty-seven acres of crown land at Ogden Point be set aside for "a public cemetery and a public market". The farmers of Saanich, "upon the occasion of the ploughing match", also prepared a resolution for the city council on the necessity of a public market. In November 1873 the meeting of citizens and city council took place. Mr. Bunster, speaking for the council, "thought that it would be no more than right for the City to have a market under the City Hall, and thereby give the farmers a chance against Chinese pedlars".

Nothing seems to have been resolved at that meeting. Undaunted, the editor of the *Colonist* a year later fastened on a new angle which ventured much further than had the council members into the murky waters of racial innuendo:

A more important object seems to be to bring producer and consumer together, so that the middlemen may no longer obliterate the margin which ought to be divided between the two great classes [producer and consumer]. . . . To this end a convenient and inexpensive public market place in this city seems essential. . . . In this way too, another class of trade infinitely more hurtful than that of the middlemen properly

so-called, and which is rapidly and almost unconsciously growing upon the community, would be cut off. We allude to Chinese hawkers, who are quietly pocketing handsome profits upon a very large part of what is consumed in this city.

In 1875, after a series of public meetings which brought no results, the editor was getting impatient with City Hall: "We hope all this wire-pulling will cease and that Council, recognizing the general desire both of producers and consumers for a market, will proceed in a straightforward way to supply the public want."

When still no progress was made, the editor pulled out all the stops in a variation of his old theme: the city needed a market for reasons of public health.

There is one argument in favour of the establishment of a public market in Victoria not to be lost sight of. The consumers of Victoria are supplied in part through Chinese who peddle their wares from house to house, to a great extent "cutting out" the legitimate producers and dealers. The vegetables hawked by these people are mostly, if not wholly raised by themselves. And how are they raised? A visit to one of the neighbourhoods of this city will effectually cure consumers of all desire to use the product thereof. The vegetables are forced to unnatural growth by the constant use of liquid manures of the most filthy character and sending forth the most abominable smells. Now, there is a high medical authority for saying that vegetables forced forward by such means are positively unwholesome. Certain it is that the smells emitted in the process of cooking are sometimes extremely offensive. Instances have been known where these odors have actually driven cooks from the kitchen. . . . If all were to meet at the public market, the consumer would soon learn to prefer the more wholesome products of the civilized farm.

The city seemed finally convinced. And a market of sorts was opened late in 1878. But no one was appeased. Writing to the *Colonist* editor, one citizen expressed his disgust with what the city had tried to fob off on the citizens as a market:

The market (?) consists of a row of shanties about 10 or 12 feet wide, without a window or awning, costing, I should say, two or three hundred dollars, and are utterly useless for any kind of market purposes. In fact, my first impression was that they were intended for water-closets, for which they seem admirably adapted.

To which the editor replied:

The quarters provided as a market are so small and inconvenient that not a single application has yet been received, and the farmers still hawk provisions from door to door seeking customers.

The ugly side of the issue surfaced again in the disappointed laments of some citizens:

The building was finished, sham stalls were erected and there the farce ended. Had the market been established as it ought . . . the consumer would no longer be imposed on by a middleman . . . and he could do his own buying and feel certain that the vegetables he had purchased had not been sweltering for hours in a filthy Chinese den to be

contaminated with disease and opium smoke, or produced by the beastly and abominable mode of culture of the Celestial race.

In 1890 things had never looked better for a successful conclusion to the market project. The citizens were coming out with suggestions and countersuggestions. Mr. De Cosmos offered to sell the city some old church property on Pandora Street for the market. The stockyards an old Fort Street were also proposed as a possible site. The editor of the *Colonist*, on the eve of the vote on the market bylaw, sent a reporter out on the streets to canvass citizens' opinions. Mr. King, a dealer in fruit and fish, said "that if the municipal authorities would stop the practice of peddling, and make everyone pay a licence, he should have no objection to take a stand in the proposed market, in which, however, he saw no special advantage". Mr. Demers, a grocer in the city, "strongly favoured the market system, as centring there everything that was required by the consumer". Mr. Cahill, "who, as everyone knows, is a typical workingman, approved the idea of a public market, though he would not force those who already occupied shops to close them and go to the market". Alderman Goodacre "expressed the opinion that it was a waste of time and expense to put up a market . . . , particularly when he saw the failure of a public market as near as Vancouver. Whence, he would like to know, would come the garden stuff to occupy one stall in the market? In the old country, indeed, many former public markets had been turned into tenements and rooms for the poor, the fact being that the idea of public markets was utterly behind that age and completely played out."

Played out or not, Victoria got its public market in 1891. Nothing small or inadequate this time. The city built the grandest market hall the country had ever seen. The editor of the *Colonist* could hardly keep his pen to the page when he described the new market:

> The structure is built of brick and splendid pieces of Nelson Island granite, which form the main arched entrances. The openings into the building are broad and high, giving ample room for the passage of vehicles of all description. There is a frontage of 210 feet and a width of 60 feet. On entering it is hard to believe that you are in a covered building, as the light is, if anything, more brilliant, because reflected, than in the open air. The whole of the roof is built of the finest cathedral glass, supported by strong but thin and shapely iron beams. There is not a single pipe visible in the whole building. . . . Two handsome ornamental fountains will be placed at equal distances away, and will add a great deal to the general effect. An ascent is made to the upper story by means of two broad, easy staircases, one at each end of the building. On reaching the gallery the visitor is struck with the light airy appearance of the whole structure, as viewed from the top. The gallery is over twenty feet wide, and forms a magnificent promenade, enclosed on the inside by handsome railings, and on the outside by a series of shops and stalls that run all round the building. At the end of the hall is a circular band stand that juts out from the balcony, commanding an excellent view. . . . On the top floor are rooms that will be reserved for lunch parlours for ladies, and general restaurants. . . . Twelve electric arc lights will be suspended from the glass roof, and besides these, of course, the stores will be furnished with gas and smaller lights.

A few months later the editor was forced to deal with the issue of "why producers and housekeepers fail to use the public trading place". Of the sixty stalls in the market hall only fourteen were occupied and by some rather unlikely characters:

> One is the studio of a teacher of painting; the city hotel makes sample rooms of some of the stalls; the Salvation Army have a band room and juvenile singing class; the Garrison artillery have an armoury, and they and the Knights of Pythias find the hall an excellent place to drill in; and a couple of grain and produce merchants do a thriving business in handling some of the articles for which it was intended that the market should be headquarters. Just at present there is a mammoth display of carpets, occupying the balcony railing on all four sides of the building, but these are salvage from a wreck, hanging up to dry . . . and the place is not regularly used for the disposal of dry goods.

There was no one reason why the market house was not being used, though the editor over the next year or so was full of suggestions. At first it seemed, he said, that farmers were afraid to come because customers might not show up, and customers were not showing up because they were not sure the farmers would come. He had one practical suggestion: "The Chinese cabins will have to be cleared off the adjoining streets before ladies can be asked to make the market their headquarters for the purchase of meat and produce."

A few years later the market was suffering "cold neglect", according to the editor. In an attempt to shame Victorians into using the market, the editor related a story told to him by a newcomer to the city who set off one morning, basket in hand, to buy a few things for dinner. "All I wanted to get was some fresh eggs and perhaps a few vegetables, but the farmers were not in evidence. I found a worn-out fire engine or two, which I had no special use for, a portrait painter's studio, a real estate agent and the sanitary inspector . . . and, most ghastly of all things—the public morgue."

After 1898 we hear no more from the editor of the *Colonist* on the subject of the market. Either he finally gave up or he died.

The market went through a series of renovations and refurbishings over the next thirty years, but nothing could be done to get the people of Victoria to use it. Only during the First World War was the building well used and for the purposes for which it was intended. After that, business tapered off and never picked up again. At one point City Council proposed turning it into a pound for stray dogs, cats and cattle. Outraged citizens put an end to that proposal, but they did not go to the market.

In 1959 City Council decided, again against protests from the citizens, to raze the building and use the land for "a more profitable purpose". There was one final protest, one the old editor of the *Colonist* would have applauded. On the market's last day, Attillio Randy, a gardener who had rented a stall in the market hall, staged a sit-down strike and sat alone in the old market for two days. No one offered to join him.

Victorians are talking again about re-establishing a public market.

# Notes

Markets in Ancient Athens and Rome
1. Athenaeus, *Deipnosophistai*, xiv; quoted in Al. N. Oikonomides, *The Two Agoras in Ancient Athens* (Chicago: Argonaut, 1964), p. 17.
2. Pollux, 9:47-48; quoted in R. E. Wycherley, *The Stones of Athens* (Princeton: Princeton University Press, 1978), p. 93.
3. Philostratus, *Life of Appollonius of Tyana*, I. 15; quoted in Paul Mac-Kendrick, *The Roman Mind at Work* (New York: Van Nostrand Reinhold, 1958).

Markets in England in the Middle Ages
1. Geoffrey Chaucer, *The Canterbury Tales*, Prologue (Harmondsworth: Penguin Books, 1960), p. 29.

The Market Tradition in Canada
1. Barry Broadfoot, *The Pioneer Years* (Toronto: PaperJacks, 1978), pp. 275-76.

Charlottetown Farmers' Market
1. Descriptions of Charlottetown's early markets are taken from T. E. MacNutt's "Charlottetown's Four Market Houses" (Public Archives of Prince Edward Island, n.d.), unpublished paper.

Halifax City Market
1. Sam Slick is the Yankee hero of Thomas Haliburton's *The Clockmaker*, published in 1837.
2. This and other quotes about Halifax's Green Market appear in D. E. Robinson's *The Halifax City Market, 1750-1977: A Special Report* (Nova Scotia Department of Agriculture and Marketing, 1978).

Markets in New Brunswick
1. Rev. J. W. Millidge, "Reminiscences of St. John from 1849 to 1860." New Brunswick Historical Society, *Collections* 4, no. 10: 131.
2. William Christopher Atkinson, *An Historical and Statistical Account of New Brunswick . . .* (Edinburgh: Anderson and Bryce, 1844), p. 108.

Markets in Quebec
1. George Munro Grant, *French Canadian Life and Character* (Chicago: Alexander Belford, 1899), p. 100.
2. Jeremy Cockloft, *Cursory Observations made in Quebec . . . in the year 1811* (Toronto: Oxford University Press, 1960) pp. 11-14.

3. William Kirby, *Reminiscences of a Visit to Quebec, July 1839* [n.p. 1903], p. 3.
4. Alfred Sandham, *Ville-Marie or, Sketches of Montreal, Past and Present* (Montreal: George Bishop, 1870), p. 200.

Toronto's St. Lawrence Market
1. Timothy Nightingale to Quetton St. George, in Edith Firth, *The Town Of York*, vol. 1 (Toronto: University of Toronto Press, 1962), pp. 134-35.
2. George Henry, "York in 1831", in Edith Firth, *The Town of York*, vol. 2 (Toronto: University of Toronto Press, 1962), p. 326.

Kitchener Farmers' Market
1. Jim Romahn, "Selling food at the market taught a lasting lesson", *Kitchener-Waterloo Record*, Kitchener's 125th Anniversary Edition, 21 June 1979.

Edmonton City Market
1. Quoted in J. G. MacGregor, *Edmonton, A History* (Edmonton: Hurtig, 1967), p. 21.
2. Ibid., pp. 48-49.
3. Barry Broadfoot, *The Pioneer Years* (Toronto: PaperJacks, 1978), p. 250.

Markets in Saskatchewan
1. Elva Fletcher, "More than the price is right", *Country Guide*, April 1976.

# Bibliography

Akins, T. B. *History of Halifax City*. 1895. Reprint, Belleville, Ont.: Mika, 1973.

Artibise, Alan. *Winnipeg, An Illustrated History*. Toronto: James Lorimer, 1977.

Atkinson, William Christopher. *An Historical and Statistical Account of New Brunswick, B.N.A., with advice to emigrants*. Edinburgh: Anderson and Bryce, 1844.

Babbitt, G. W. *Fredericton in the Eighties, with glimpses of St. John, Moncton, and St. Andrews*. Toronto: Babbitt, 1950.

Bennett, Thomas A. "Direct Marketing of Fresh Fruits and Vegetables—A Look at Farmers' Markets in Canada". *Canadian Farm Economics* 9, no. 5 (1975): 1-8.

Broadfoot, Barry. *The Pioneer Years 1895-1914: Memories of Settlers Who Opened the West*. Reprint. Toronto: PaperJacks, 1978.

Campbell, Patrick. *Travels in the Interior Inhabited Parts of North America, in the years 1791 and 1792*. Reprint. Toronto: Champlain Society, 1937.

Careless, J. M. S., ed. *Colonists and Canadiens, 1760-1867*. Toronto: Macmillan, 1971.

Chaucer, Geoffrey. *The Canterbury Tales*. Reprint. Harmondsworth: Penguin Books, 1960.

Clark, Andrew Hill. *Three Centuries and the Island: A Historical Geography of Settlement and Agriculture in Prince Edward Island*. Toronto: University of Toronto Press, 1959.

Clark, C. *The Economics of Subsistence Agriculture*. London: Macmillan, 1970.

Cockloft, Jeremy. *Cursory Observations made in Quebec, Province of Lower Canada, in the year 1811*. Reprint. Toronto: Oxford University Press, 1960.

Davis, Dorothy. *Fairs, Shops and Supermarkets*. Toronto: University of Toronto Press, 1966.

Defoe, Daniel. *The Compleat English Tradesman*. Reprint. New York: B. Franklin, 1970.

Dickens, Charles. *American Notes*. Reprint. London: Dent, 1908.

Dickinson, R. E. "The Markets and Market Area of Bury St. Edmonds". *Sociological Review* 22 (1930): 292-308.

Easterbrook. W. T. and Watkins, M. H., eds. *Approaches to Canadian Economic History*. Toronto: Macmillan, 1967.

Finley, M. I. *The Ancient Economy*. Berkeley, Calif.: University of California Press, 1973.

Finley, M. I., ed. *Studies in Ancient Society*. London: Routledge Kegan, Paul, 1974.

Firth, Edith, ed. *The Town of York: A Collection of Documents of Early Toronto*. 2 vols. Toronto: University of Toronto Press, 1962.

Fisher, F. J. "The Development of the London Food Market, 1540-1640". *Economic History Review* 5 (1935).

Fletcher, Elva. "More than the price is right". *Country Guide*, April 1976, pp. 22-26.

Grant, George Munro. *French Canadian Life and Character*. Chicago: Alexander Belford, 1899.

Gras, Norman. *A History of Agriculture in Europe and America*. 2nd ed. New York: F. S. Crofts, 1946.

_____. *The Economic and Social History of an English Village*. Reprint. New York: Russell & Russell, 1969.

Greenhill, Basil and Gifford, Ann. *Westcountrymen in Prince Edward's Isle*. Toronto: University of Toronto Press, 1967.

Gregson, H. *A History of Victoria*. Vancouver: J. J. Douglas, 1977.

Guillett, E. C. *Early Life in Upper Canada*. Toronto: University of Toronto Press, 1963.

_____. *The Pioneer Farmer and Backwoodsman*. 2 vols. Toronto: University of Toronto Press, 1963.

Haliburton, Thomas Chandler. *The Clockmaker; or the sayings and doings of Samuel Slick of Slicksville*. Reprint. Toronto: McClelland and Stewart, 1958.

_____. *History of Nova Scotia*. 1829. Reprint. 2 vols. Belleville. Ont.: Mika, 1973.

Heilbroner, R. L. *The Making of Economic Society*. Englewood Cliffs, N. J.: Prentice Hall, 1968.

Homer, Robert and Beverly Neish. *Report to the British Columbia Ministry of Agriculture on Farmers' Markets.* Vancouver: B.C. Ministry of Agriculture, 1979.

Hoyt, E. E. *Primitive Trade: Its Psychology and Economics.* New York: Augustus M. Kelley, 1968.

Huggett, Renee. *Shops.* London: B. T. Batsford, 1969.

Innis, H. A. *Essays in Canadian Economic History.* Toronto: University of Toronto Press, 1956.

Jones, R. L. *History of Agriculture in Ontario, 1613-1880.* Reprint. Toronto: University of Toronto Press, 1977.

Kerridge, E. *The Agricultural Revolution.* London: Allen and Unwin, 1967.

Kirby, William. *Reminiscences of a Visit to Quebec, July 1839.* [n.p. 1903].

Lopez, L. S. *The Commercial Revolution of the Middle Ages, 950-1350.* Englewood Cliffs, N.J.: Prentice-Hall, 1971.

Lower, A. R. M. *Colony to Nation.* Toronto: McClelland and Stewart, 1977.

MacEwan, J. W. G. *Agriculture on Parade: Fairs and Exhibitions in Western Canada.* Toronto: Nelson, 1950.

————. *Between the Red and the Rockies.* Saskatoon: Western Producer Prairie Books, 1979.

MacGregor, J. G. *Edmonton, A History.* Edmonton: Hurtig, 1967.

McKendrick, Paul. *The Roman Mind at Work.* New York: Van Nostrand Reinhold, 1958.

MacMullen, Ramsay. "Market-days in the Roman Empire". *Phoenix* 24 (1970) : 333-341.

MacNutt, T. E. "Charlottetown's Four Market Houses". Public Archives of Prince Edward Island, n.d. Unpublished paper.

MacNutt, W. S. *The Atlantic Provinces, 1713-1857.* Toronto: McClelland and Stewart, 1965.

Millidge, Rev. J. W. "Reminiscences of St. John from 1849-1860". New Brunswick Historical Society. *Collections* 4, no. 10: 126-135.

Montet, Pierre. *Everyday Life in Egypt.* Reprint. Westport, Conn.: Greenwood Press, 1974.

Morley, Alan. *Vancouver, Milltown to Metropolis.* Vancouver: Mitchell Press, 1974.

Mund, Vernon. *Open Markets.* New York: Harper and Row, 1948.

Nicol, Eric. *Vancouver.* Toronto: Doubleday, 1978.

Oikonomides, Al. N. *The Two Agoras in Athens.* Chicago: Argonaut, 1964.

Ontario Association of Agricultural Societies. *The Story of Ontario's Agricultural Fairs and Exhibitions, 1792-1967.* Toronto: Ontario Association of Agricultural Societies, 1967.

Platt, Colin. *The English Medieval Town.* New York: David McKay, 1976.

Power, E. *Medieval People.* London: Methuen, 1964.

Power, E. and Postan, M. M. *English Trade in the Fifteenth Century.* London: Methuen, 1967.

Raddall, Thomas H. *Halifax: Warden of the North.* Toronto: McClelland and Stewart, 1948.

Reaman, Elmore. *A History of Agriculture in Ontario.* Toronto: Saunders, 1969.

Roberts, L. *Montreal: From Mission Colony to World City.* Toronto: Macmillan, 1969.

Robinson, D. E. *The Halifax City Market, 1750-1977: A Special Report.* Halifax: Nova Scotia Department of Agriculture and Marketing, 1978.

Rostovtzeff, M. *Rome.* London: Oxford University Press, 1960.

Salzman, L. F. *English Life in the Middle Ages.* London: Oxford University Press, 1929.

————. *English Trade in the Middle Ages.* London: Clarendon Press, 1931.

Sandham, Alfred. *Ville-Marie or, Sketches of Montreal, Past and Present.* Montreal: George Bishop, 1870.

Straever, Stuart, ed. *Prehistoric Agriculture.* New York: Natural History, 1971.

Tannahill, R. *Food in History.* London: Methuen, 1973.

Thirsk, Joan. "Seventeenth Century Agriculture and Social Change". *The Agricultural History Review* 18 (1970): 148-177.

Tremblay, Marc-Adelard. *Rural Canada in Transition.* Publication no. 6. Ottawa: Agricultural Economics Research Council of Canada, 1966.

Uttley, W. V. *A history of Kitchener, Ontario.* Reprint. Waterloo: Wilfrid Laurier University Press, 1975.

Waite, P. B., ed. *Pre Confederation.* Scarborough, Ont.: Prentice-Hall of Canada, 1965.

Waterbury, David H. "Retrospective Rambles over Historic St. John, 1849-1860". New Brunswick Historical Society. *Collections* 4, no. 10: 86-103.

Westerfield, R. *Middlemen in English Business.* 1915. Reprint. New York: Augustus M. Kelley, 1968.

White, K.D. *Country Life in Classical Times.* New York: Cornell University, 1977.

————. *Roman Farming.* London: Thames and Hudson, 1970.

Wood, R. *The Agrarian Myth in Canada*. Toronto: McClelland and Stewart, 1975.

Wright, E. *The Loyalists of New Brunswick*. Wolfville, N.S.: Wright, 1955.

Wycherley, R. E. *The Stones of Athens*. Princeton: Princeton University Press, 1978.

# Picture Credits

Royal Ontario Museum  13
Prince Edward Island Public Archives  23, 30, 32, 33
Mary Ann LaPierre  44, 48
Nova Scotia Archives  45
Ontario Archives  50, 72 *right*
New Brunswick Museum  54
New Brunswick Archives  64
Public Archives Canada  72 *left*, 74, 80, 119
City of Toronto Archives  88, 89, 90
Kitchener Waterloo Record  102
City of Edmonton Archives  128, 129
Victoria City Archives  150, 152

All other photographs are by J. Douglas Wilson, except for those of the
Granville Island Market, Vancouver, which are by Yvonne Grue.

# Index